JESUS' COPERNICAN REVOLUTION

The Revelation of Divine Mercy

JESUS' COPERNICAN REVOLUTION

The Revelation of Divine Mercy

James P. Danaher

PARAGON HOUSE

First Edition 2016

Published in the United States by
Paragon House
Saint Paul, Minnesota

www.ParagonHouse.com

Bible references from the New Revised Standard Version unless otherwise noted.

Library of Congress Cataloging-in-Publication Data

Danaher, James P.
Jesus' Copernican revolution : the revelation of divine mercy / James P. Danaher.
-- First Edition.
pages cm
Summary: "Jesus offered a revolutionary way to view the world, showing that we must abandon our cultural and religious prejudices to reach higher levels of consciousness, and incarnate a divine mercy that leads to peace"-- Provided by publisher.
ISBN 978-1-55778-918-1 (pbk. : alk. paper) 1. Jesus Christ--Teachings. 2. Christianity--Philosophy. 3. Christian philosophy. I. Title.
BS2415.D36 2015
232.9'54--dc23
2015018327

Manufactured in the United States of America

10 9 8 7 6 5 4 3 2 1

The paper used in this publication meets the minimum requirements of American National Standard for Information Sciences—Permanence of Paper for Printed Library Materials, ANSIZ39.48-1984.

For my father
James Patrick Danaher, Sr.

"What manner of man is this,
that even the wind and the sea obey him?"

—Mark 4:41

Acknowledgment

I would like to acknowledge my gratitude to my editor, Janna Kasarjian, my proofreader, Willard Pottinger, and my research assistant, Erik Salvesen. Their contributions have been great and so is my gratitude.

Contents

Preface

According to the Pew Forum of Religion and Public Life, people who consider themselves Christians are divided into more than 40,000 denominations worldwide. How can such enormous diversity come out of reading the same book? The answer is really quite simple. Since the Bible does not contain italics, we get to decide where to put the emphasis. For example, let me paint a scenario for you. Imagine two people in the midst of a heated argument, and the one utters to the other, "I never said you stole the money." We might think that this is a fairly straight forward statement, but the meaning changes depending upon where we place the emphasis. If we emphasize the fact that ***I*** was not the one that said you stole the money, it implies that someone else said it. By contrast, "I never ***said*** you stole the money," means I might have implied it, but I never said it; while "I never said ***you*** stole the money," means someone else stole the money. Other readings which put the emphasis on "stole" or "money" give very different meanings. "I never said you ***stole*** the money," means you somehow ended up with the money, or "I never said you stole the ***money,***" means you stole something else. One sentence can have five different meanings depending upon where the emphasis is placed. Now consider the enormous number of sentences in the Bible, and it becomes clear why there are over 40,000 Christian denominations. Depending upon our individual prejudices, coupled with those we inherit from our particular history, culture, and language community, we place the emphasis in a multitude of varying places, giving the Bible texts countless different meanings.

Over the last two centuries, we have arrived at a far greater knowledge regarding our human experience. We do not record data simply as given; instead, we interpret the data of our experience according to the unique way our species has been equipped to process those data. No animal species perceives the world as it is, but rather as its particular species has been equipped to perceive it. Aristotle was the first to write about the five senses through which human beings have access to the world. That is our limited access, but the scientific study of how different animal species perceive the world reveals that many animals have senses that go far beyond our five limited senses. Thus, many animals are aware of a world to which we are oblivious.

Even our own limited perception of the world is more about what is inside of us rather than what is out there in the world. In the words of an ophthalmologist, "The eye doesn't see. The brain sees. The eye just transmits." The brain literally tells us what to see and what it tells us is based upon how our brains have been trained and educated to interpret reality. Thus, what we see isn't simply determined by what comes through the eyes. What we see is both affected and effected by our memories, feelings, and, most importantly, how we have been taught to interpret the data of our experience. This is why magicians can do what they do. We think we know what we see, but the brain tells us what to see and that isn't always what is *there* but rather what is in us. These are the prejudices that so greatly shape our experience and make human experience so different from that of the animal kingdom. We live in a world that has been socially constructed; the rest of the animal kingdom processes the data of its experience through the cognitive hardware with which nature has provided it. Of course, we human beings also have a natural cognitive hardware unique to our species, but in addition to that we also process much of the data of our experience through concepts that were shaped by the judgments and conventions of past generations. This is the mind we inherit from our specific culture, history, and language community. Thus, human experience is enormously diverse, yet whenever people agree upon some social construct they all too easily assume it to be part of the objective world rather than part of their own vision. Race is a social construct invented five hundred years ago. Once created, however, we naively suppose that race is part of objective reality, rather than the way we have been taught to perceive reality. Most of the concepts through which we conceptualize the world are social constructs and not part of the innate hardware common to our species. These concepts and the meaning we attribute to them provide the prejudices through which we interpret everything, even the Gospel.

Most of us are oblivious to this. Instead, we naively assume that our reading is based upon what is in the text rather than what is in us. When we hear Jesus talk about things like law, love, truth, family, sin, faith, or religion, we assume we know what he is talking about because we are familiar with such concepts. Scholars, however, tell us that our concepts of such things are not necessarily those of a Palestinian Jew of two thousand years ago. Scholars try to overcome this difficulty by studying the ancient languages and cultures from which a work such as the Gospel would have emanated. That sounds like a good strategy, unless we are up against a Copernican revolution, the likes of which the world had never seen.

CHAPTER ONE

Jesus' Copernican Revolution

FIVE HUNDRED YEARS ago, Nicolaus Copernicus (1473-1543) introduced a radically new way to perceive the universe. Despite the benefits of this contribution, the perspective that he was introducing went against such a deeply-held prejudice that it was almost unanimously rejected. It seemed obvious to nearly everyone that the earth was larger and immobile in comparison to the sun, and therefore it was the sun that was moving and not the earth. Eventually, Copernicus convinced us of a better way to conceptualize and interpret this, but for most people the natural prejudice that stood in their way took quite some time to overcome, and for some it still persists. A recent survey by the National Science Foundation found that one in four Americans still believe that the sun revolves around the earth.

We see the world in a certain way and we think of it as an objective fact, but that is very often simply a prejudice about the way we learned to conceptualize the world. Human beings think that they know all sorts of things, but many of those things are really the result of prejudices. When a deep prejudice is exposed and we learn to think about a certain thing differently, we refer to that as a Copernican revolution.

The eighteenth century German philosopher Immanuel Kant

(1724-1804) had his own Copernican revolution. Until Kant, most people believed that our experience was simply a matter of recording data as given. It was Kant's revolutionary thinking that brought us to realize that our experience was actually a composite of both the data of our experience and the understanding through which we interpret the data. Sadly, just as many Americans are unaware of Copernicus and his revolution, an even greater percentage are unaware of Kant's revolution. Many people still believe that what they perceive is objective reality, rather than an interpretation.

Some revolutions concerning our thinking have been more easily adapted simply because they were not confronted by such deeply-held prejudices. Several hundred years ago, nearly everyone accepted the notion that the "divine right of kings" was the basis for legitimate political authority. Few people subscribe to that belief today and, at least in democratic cultures, we now maintain that legitimacy in terms of political power comes through the consent of the governed. Similarly, Isaac Newton (1643-1727) ushered in a new way to conceptualize the world as mechanical rather than biological, and many within the scientific community quickly saw a benefit to this way of conceptualizing the world.

Of course, there have been unsuccessful Copernican revolutions. Some failed because they simply did not provide a better way to interpret our experience, but what about a Copernican revolution that did offer a better way to interpret our experience, but in doing so it went up against numerous prejudices that we held as sacred? Such a person wouldn't have much of a chance of getting their perspective accepted even if they were able to work unbelievable miracles. We may be open to changing our thinking here and there but not when it comes to those ideas we hold as most cherished. And if there are numerous challenges to those precious concepts, such thinking is immediately dismissed or ignored.

The major reason for this is that we hold the inherited understanding through which we interpret our experience as both true and even sacred. There are several reasons for this. As children, we have no basis from which to reject our initial orientation to the world. Furthermore, it is necessary for our psychological development and social wellbeing that we embrace our initial conceptual understanding as true. Even later in life, we get a great sense of security from believing that our way of interpreting our experience is sacred. Consider the response to the civil rights movement by segregationists in the American south during the 1960s. The concept of segregation had been learned at their mother's knee, and they held it as a sacred concept. They saw it as an objective truth, rather than simply the way they had been taught to interpret things.

Of course, our response when someone challenges our sacred concepts is not always violent as it was with the segregationists. Sometimes we simply ignore a new conceptualization or dismiss it as ridiculous. With the radical concepts Jesus introduces we have several strategies. Either we argue that Jesus really doesn't mean what he says and spin his words into something more compatible with our inherited understanding, or simply ignore his teachings completely and focus on other portions of the Bible that offer a perspective more compatible with our own.

We much prefer to read the Gospel through our prejudices rather than attempt to take on the mind of Christ by letting the things Jesus says and does do violence to those valued prejudices that comprise our conceptual understanding.

This book is about the revolutionary perspective that Jesus offered, but two thousand years later his "followers" are still filtering his message through social and cultural prejudices that turn his words into something far less radical than the divine perspective he was offering. A primary prejudice behind this is the belief that, if we are made in God's image, God must be like us and love what we love and hate what we hate. What we actually see in the Jesus revelation, however, is something quite different; what God loves is as different from what we imagine, as Copernicus' idea of a heliocentric universe is from a geocentric universe.

A Copernican revolution is most easily accomplished if it challenges prejudices to which people are not deeply committed, but Jesus' teachings tell us that we are wrong about the sacred prejudices we hold toward things like righteousness, justice, wealth, and family. Those are the teachings we ignore. We want to read the Jesus message by emphasizing those things he says that agree with our prejudices, and we want to ignore the radical things he says that threaten our prejudices.

Christian theology has largely ignored Jesus' teachings and made the Gospel into something we can live with rather than something that transforms us. Most people are not interested in transformation into a new kind of being, but want religions that are compatible with, and reinforce, their inherited understanding. That was the nature of the devoutly religious people in Jesus' time, and it is still the nature of most religious types today. In short, we want a God who will save us, not one who will change us. In fact, we reject the God Jesus presents and, like the older brother in the story of the prodigal, resent a father who loves the prodigal as much as the good son. We want a more human God who loves in proportion to our righteousness, but Jesus tells us none are righteous, and all must come through repentance and the experience of God's mercy. That is simply too contrary to some of our deepest prejudices. So we retain our cultural concepts of righteousness, justice, sin, faith, and love, and ignore the revolutionary perspective Jesus offers.

We are not interested in the Jesus perspective, but instead seek comprehensive theologies that purport to give us objective truth. This is the great difference today between those who consider themselves Christians. It is not a denominational difference between Catholics and Protestants, but between those who see their Christianity as a matter of believing in a theology that is objectively true, and those who seek to take on the mind of Christ and see the world through Jesus' conceptual understanding. The Jesus perspective is not a theology but a way to conceptualize the world. Unfortunately, we choose instead theologies that we not only can grasp, but from which we derive a sense of security by believing that they represent objective truth. Of course, they do not. They are theories that represent the human perspectives of Thomas Aquinas, Martin Luther, or John Calvin, but we are much more comfortable with those perspectives than the divine perspective that Jesus offers.

Jesus never wrote a long treatise explaining and defending his radical perspective the way Copernicus and Kant did. Of course, we have the Gospels; however, we persist in reading them through our own cherished concepts. If only we would allow Jesus' words to do violence to our prejudices, we might then come closer to the mind of Christ—through which to perceive God, the world, and ourselves.

Initially, we read everything through our cultural and linguistic prejudices. We achieve higher levels of consciousness as those prejudices are exposed and we move beyond them. Copernicus and Kant offered a better way to see the world. Jesus also offered us a higher level of consciousness but it is simply *too* high for us. It is a divine perspective and therefore threatens to destroy too many of our sacred human prejudices. So we worship Jesus as God, in order to feel justified at ignoring that to which he calls us. We tell ourselves that since he is God, we cannot ascend to his level of consciousness as it is out of reach and beyond our human potential. And, indeed, it is. But he calls us to pursue it in order that our failure to achieve it will bring us to the experience of God's mercy, and it is the repeated experience of mercy that in time begins to make us into his merciful likeness.

CHAPTER TWO

Jesus on Religion

IT IS IRONIC THAT we made Jesus into a religion, since the people Jesus found most troublesome were those who were devoutly religious. He was kind and merciful to all the repentant sinners, but he rebuked those who thought that their religious tradition made them righteous. Religious people have not changed much in the last two thousand years. They still believe they find favor with God through their religious beliefs, sinless behavior, or rituals, but Jesus tells us that our attempts at such righteousness are ultimately futile and all must come through God's mercy. Of course, people who think they have the right beliefs, behavior, or rituals don't want to be told that they are in need of mercy; nor do they want to extend mercy to others who do not share their claim to righteousness.

Consequently, many religious people who consider themselves Christians pay little attention to Jesus' teachings, and instead create theologies that assure them that they have been made righteous and are no longer in need of mercy. This all too easily happens because of our seemingly natural prejudice toward righteousness. Doesn't God want us to be good? Our theologies tell us how to be good in God's sight. Jesus, however, tells us that we are not good and in fact God desires us to be merciful rather than righteous. He constantly undermines the notion that we can find favor with God through our righteousness and instead points us toward mercy. Consider Jesus' interaction with a lawyer which leads to the parable of the Good Samaritan.

> Just then a lawyer stood up to test Jesus. "Teacher," he said, "what must I do to inherit eternal life?" He said to him, "What is written in the law? What do you read there?" He answered, "You shall love the Lord your God with all your heart, and with all your soul, and with all your strength, and with all your mind; and your neighbor as yourself." And he said to him, "You have given the right answer; do this, and you will live."[1]

Notice there is nothing here about the avoidance of sin or right religious doctrine. It is about loving God and your neighbor. Jesus' teachings are all about how to love God and how to love others as ourselves, rather than the avoidance of sin. In fact, the parable goes on to make this very point.

> But wanting to justify himself, he asked Jesus, "And who is my neighbor?" Jesus replied, "A man was going down from Jerusalem to Jericho, and fell into the hands of robbers, who stripped him, beat him, and went away, leaving him half dead. Now by chance a priest was going down that road; and when he saw him, he passed by on the other side. So likewise a Levite, when he came to the place and saw him, passed by on the other side. But a Samaritan while traveling came near him; and when he saw him, he was moved with pity. He went to him and bandaged his wounds, having poured oil and wine

1. Luke 10:25-28.

> on them. Then he put him on his own animal, brought him to an inn, and took care of him. The next day he took out two denarii, gave them to the innkeeper, and said, 'Take care of him; and when I come back, I will repay you whatever more you spend.' Which of these three, do you think, was a neighbor to the man who fell into the hands of the robbers?" He said, "The one who showed him mercy." Jesus said to him, "Go and do likewise."[2]

Jesus consistently condemns our pretense to righteousness and tells us instead to be merciful as God is merciful. Notice how both the priest and the Levite avoid the man in the ditch. In their theology the man must be a sinner to have fallen into such a terrible state. Righteous people today often share the same perspective. The homeless are in the state that they are in because of their sin of addiction, or laziness, or the like. Why should their sin be rewarded? This is the thinking of the righteous, but a third man appears in the story who is not a good, religious man. He is despised by the religious people of Jesus' day. He is a Samaritan and does not have the right theology. He doesn't believe the right things and therefore cannot be right with God. But Jesus flips this notion upside down and tells us of a God who first and foremost desires that we would be merciful as he is merciful. As Jesus says in other places, "Go and learn what this means, 'I desire mercy and not sacrifice.'"[3]

The main point of this parable is that our love is terribly limited. That is what the lawyer is asking of Jesus: how far does my love have to extend? Who is my neighbor? I have to love those

2. Luke 10:29-37.
3. Matthew 9:13.

of my own tribe, but what about the people on the other side of the river? Certainly, they are not my neighbors. The lawyer wants Jesus to define where people stop being a neighbor and thus he no longer has to love them. In typical Jesus fashion, Jesus doesn't answer that question, but instead chooses someone whom a good Jew of two thousand years ago would never have considered his neighbor. Jesus is taking us beyond the tribalism from which all religion begins and is showing us a God who is much more than we care to imagine. We much prefer a righteous God who demands righteousness from his people rather than a God of infinite mercy. A God of infinite mercy would have us extend mercy even to our enemies, and that is not a God we want.

Nearly all of the theologies that have been produced by Christians over the last two thousand years have been about what to believe and what not to do in order to be right with God, but Jesus tells us that we are already right with God because of God's mercy, and his desire is simply that we would become merciful as he is merciful. In the twenty-fifth chapter of Matthew's Gospel Jesus tells an amazing story about the sheep and the goats.

> "When the Son of Man comes in His glory, and all the holy angels with Him, then He will sit on the throne of His glory. All the nations will be gathered before Him, and He will separate them one from another, as a shepherd divides his sheep from the goats. And He will set the sheep on His right hand, but the goats on the left. Then the King will say to those on His right hand, 'Come, you blessed of My Father, inherit the kingdom prepared for you from the foundation of the world: for I was hungry and you gave Me food; I was thirsty and you gave Me drink; I was a stranger and you took Me in; I *was*

> naked and you clothed Me; I was sick and you visited Me; I was in prison and you came to Me.' Then the righteous will answer Him, saying, 'Lord, when did we see You hungry and feed You, or thirsty and give You drink? When did we see You a stranger and take You in, or naked and clothe You? Or when did we see You sick, or in prison, and come to You?' And the King will answer and say to them, 'Assuredly, I say to you, inasmuch as you did it to one of the least of these My brethren, you did it to Me.' Then He will also say to those on the left hand, 'Depart from Me, you cursed, into the everlasting fire prepared for the devil and his angels: for I was hungry and you gave Me no food; I was thirsty and you gave Me no drink; I was a stranger and you did not take Me in, naked and you did not clothe Me, sick and in prison and you did not visit Me.' Then they also will answer Him, saying, 'Lord, when did we see You hungry or thirsty or a stranger or naked or sick or in prison, and did not minister to You?' Then He will answer them, saying, 'Assuredly, I say to you, inasmuch as you did not do it to one of the least of these, you did not do it to Me.' "[4]

How do we see this as religious? Today, religions are belief systems that separate people into different tribal groups. By contrast, the story Jesus tells above has nothing to do with people's theologies or whether they even believe that God exists or not. It is about mercy. This is what we hate about Jesus, and why we pay almost no attention to his teachings. We want religions that confirm that we are righteous—that our behavior and beliefs are pleasing to God—but Jesus tells us that God is preparing a kingdom for those who are full of mercy.

---

4. Matthew 25:31-45 NKJV.

Jesus never gives us what we want in terms of theology. We want a theology by which we can feel righteous, but Jesus never gives us a theology. Theologies have to be created years later by those who consider themselves his followers. A third-year seminary student was once asked by a first-year seminary student, "How come in seminary they never talk about Jesus, just Paul?" The older student responded, "You can't make theology out of Jesus." How true! It is very difficult to align a theology that fits the Western tradition with what Jesus says. We want him to reinforce our tribal beliefs and prejudices in order to feel confident in what we know, but he never does that. Instead, his teachings are essentially assaults upon our ideas of righteousness, justice, sin, and the good life. For that reason, therefore, we pay almost no attention to his teachings. Instead, we focus on the last three days of his life where there are no teachings and we are therefore free to make up theologies to our liking. The only clue that Jesus gives concerning the meaning of his death and resurrection is when he tells us that he came "to give his life a ransom for many."[5]

Of course, he never tells us to whom the ransom is paid or what it is for, so multiple theories developed. The early theories that dominated the first thousand years of Christianity stemmed from the idea that a ransom needed to be paid to Satan. This view of atonement was referred to as *Christus Victor,* and can be traced to the early church fathers Origin and Gregory of Nyssa. In one version of *Christus Victor*, Satan held all human beings captive, but God handed Jesus over to Satan as a payment or ransom.[6]

5. Matthew 20:28, and Mark 10:45.

6. Weaver, Denny J. "Violence in Christian Theology." *Cross Currents.* Vol. 51, No. 2 (2001): 151.

According to this view, Satan had a right to do what he wished to human beings because he had taken ownership of them through the sin of Adam. Thus, if God used violence to set Satan's captives free,

> God would have been doing unjust violence against the devil, since the latter was the lawful possessor of man; for the devil had not gained his hold over man with violence rather it was man who had gone over to the devil of his own free will.[7]

The theory went on to say that with the death of Jesus, Satan had become a murderer for the first time, since Jesus was not descended from Adam who had enslaved all of his offspring due to his sin. Therefore, Satan was not the lawful possessor of Jesus and his murder of Jesus put Satan under God's judgment. Another version of *Christus Victor* depicts a battle between God and the forces of evil. In the battle, God's son is killed, but God raises him from the dead and thus defeats Satan.[8]

In the eleventh century, Anselm, the Archbishop of Canterbury (1033-1109), objected to this view and argued that the traditional idea that the ransom was paid to Satan was a mistake, and that the payment was to God, and not the devil. According to Anselm's theory, God's honor was offended by sin and Jesus' death was necessary in order to satisfy God's offended honor. For Anselm, God's honor is at the heart of his atonement theory. His is a regal notion of God consistent with the medieval prejudice that saw kingship as noble and admirable. We no longer are under

7. Anselm. *The Major Works*. Eds. Brian Davies & G. R. Evans. New York: Oxford University Press, 1998: 272.

8. Weaver, 151.

such a social prejudice, and the divine right of kings has been replaced by "rule through the consent of the governed." A kingly god whose honor is so great that he would torture his own son is no longer a god we see as worthy of worship. We might be able to muster obedience to such a god, but not love or worship. Anselm's theory leaves us with a punitive God rather than the merciful God depicted by Jesus in the Gospels. Of course, Anselm's concept of god could be worshipped by a level of consciousness that worships ideas of righteousness, power, and honor. Those possessing a level of consciousness which sees God torturing Jesus for our sins would have little problem burning heretics alive or killing the infidel through Christian Crusades or Muslim Jihads.

In the medieval world, atonement theories were put forth by others, such as Peter Abelard and Duns Scotus, but both Thomas Aquinas and the reformers accepted Anselm's theory of atonement. The reformers added the idea that divine law required punishment for sin, and Jesus agreed to suffer that punishment in man's place.[9] Since both Thomas Aquinas and the reformers endorsed Anselm's theory, it became the view of both mainstream Protestantism and Catholicism. Over the last two centuries, however, there has been opposition to that dominant view.

Of course, sins must be paid for: when the guilty pay for their sins it is called justice, but when the innocent pay for the sins of the guilty it is called forgiveness. In fact, that is the definition of forgiveness: the innocent, offended one suffers the offense without retaliation in order to restore relationship with the guilty. The most beautiful picture of divine forgiveness is Jesus responding

9. Ibid.

to the barbaric evil of crucifixion with forgiveness for his torturers.[10] Of course, to see the beauty in this we have to ascend to the higher, more divine level of consciousness that Jesus reveals throughout the Gospels. The barbaric level of consciousness will always see God doing the torturing in order to justify our own torturing of others.

Alternatives to Anselm's theory are not new. The revivalists of the 19th century were "embarrassed by the Calvinistic doctrine of penal substitution,"[11] which leaves us with a god whose honor is greater than his love for his son—a god who must be appeased even at the cost of his son's life. This view which emphasizes God's honor undermines the greatness of God's love. It gives us a picture of an exacting god who not only doesn't love us, but in fact must be placated. Consequently, some 19th century theologians rejected the idea that the atonement was a matter of God's wrath.[12] Paul Peter Waldenstrom held the view that the fall of man took place in man alone,[13] and that "the fall of man did not cause any change in the heart of God."[14] Sin is a matter of human beings turning away from God, but sin does not cause God to turn away from human beings, so there was no need for restoration on God's part. In fact, "the atonement reveals God's presence with us in

10. Luke 23:34.

11. Hicks, John Mark. "What Did Christ Accomplish on the Cross? Atonement in Campbell, Stone, and Scott." *Lexington Theological Quarterly.* Vol. 30 (Fall, 1995): 154.

12. Ibid., 145-146.

13. Gustafson, David M. "J. G. Princell and the Waldenstromian View of the Atonement." *Trinity Journal.* Vol. 20, No. 2 (1999): 192.

14. Ibid.

our sinfulness."[15] This is a very different perspective from seeing atonement as involving "some inability on God's part to look upon the sins borne by Christ."[16] When Jesus cries out, "My God, my God, why have you forsaken me?"[17] I hope we realize that what he is revealing as abandonment by God is what every human being realizes when they are in their most difficult hour. It is perhaps best described by the now-famous poem about the footsteps in the sand.

> One night I dreamed a dream. I was walking along the beach with my Lord. Across the dark sky flashed scenes from my life. For each scene, I noticed two sets of footprints in the sand, one belonging to me and one to my Lord. When the last scene of my life shot before me I looked back at the footprints in the sand. There was only one set of footprints. I realized that this was at the lowest and saddest times of my life. This always bothered me and I questioned the Lord about my dilemma. "Lord, You told me when I decided to follow You, You would walk and talk with me all the way. But I'm aware that during the most troublesome times of my life there is only one set of footprints. I just don't understand why, when I need You most, You leave me." He whispered, "My precious child, I love you and will never leave you, never, ever, during your trials and testings. When you saw only one set of footprints, it was then that I carried you."[18]

15. Duff, Nancy J. "Atonement and the Christian Life." *Interpretations*. Vol. 53, No. 1 (1999): 30.
16. Ibid.
17. Matthew 27:46.
18. Margaret Fishback Powers, 1964. Originally penned by Mary Stevenson, 1936.

This is a much better explanation for Jesus having said, "My God, my God, why have you forsaken me?" Jesus is revealing what all human beings experience in their darkest hour. It is Jesus revealing what he is experiencing and not what his Father is actually doing. Christian theology maintains that God is a triune existence, and to imagine that one of those three persons is doing violence to another one of those persons leaves us with a schizophrenic God. We have to believe that when Jesus suffers, all three persons of the Godhead suffer. So it makes much more sense to see Jesus suffering the wrath of human beings and showing us God's forgiving response to such evil, as Jesus prays for his torturers to be forgiven.[19]

Nevertheless, we are still left with the question of the ransom or payment of which Jesus speaks. Of course, it could be argued that the ransom is the payment that forgiveness necessitates. When one person does harm to another, and the relationship between them is damaged or destroyed, someone must bear the brunt if that relationship is to be restored. There is, however, an option concerning who will pay for the offense. With justice, the guilty pay for the harm they have done to the innocent and to the relationship. In some cases, justice may bring restoration to a relationship. The other option is for the innocent, who has suffered the harm, to be willing to absorb that hurt and not demand retribution. In such a circumstance, a payment is in fact made, but it is not to a specific person, but is rather the payment that forgiveness requires.

Imagine someone taking a friend's credit card without permission and using it to go on an expensive vacation. In realizing

19. Luke 23:34.

that the thousands of dollars this person had charged to his friend's account has hurt his friend and damaged his relationship with that friend, the offender experiences regret and wishes to restore the relationship. Justice would demand that the offending party compensate his friend for the injustice he has done. In some cases that might restore the relationship. If, however, the offender is unable to compensate his friend and pay back the money, the only other possible means of restoring the relationship is through the act of forgiveness. In restoring the relationship through forgiveness, the innocent must be willing to pay for what has been charged to his account and no longer treat the friend as guilty. Thus, in a sense, forgiveness is also the fulfillment of justice in that someone has paid for the offense. This is the ransom or payment that Jesus makes on behalf of God and not on behalf of human beings. The Cross is a picture of divine forgiveness.

Another way to understand what happened on the Cross is by considering the example of adultery. Imagine a love relationship where one person is hurt by the other person's infidelity. Harm has been done to the relationship, but the innocent is willing to suffer the harm and therein pay the price of restoring the relationship. In fact, the relationship may be better than ever if the guilty party fully appreciates that the innocent one cherishes the relationship enough to pay dearly to preserve it. Of course, the situation is quite different for the innocent one who must do the forgiving. A person in this position must calculate whether the desire to restore the relationship to its previous state is worth the enormous pain that must be endured to do so. When most of us make such a calculation, we are only willing to forgive if we judge the hurt to be something we can bear. If we think the offense is unbearable, we choose not to restore the relationship, and by so doing we equally choose not to forgive. What Jesus reveals from the Cross is that the Divine is always willing to endure enormous suffering in order to restore relationship—even relationship with his torturers.

Reminiscent of what Jesus reveals on the Cross is a story about a woman who had been raped and her entire family killed by a gang of soldiers. Years later, while working as a nurse, a soldier was brought to her hospital on the brink of death. The nurse recognized him as the officer in charge of the men who raped her and killed her family. After eight days the man had been nursed back to health by this woman and, upon regaining consciousness, he was told that the only reason he was alive was because of the loving care of this woman. Upon recognizing her, he was taken back, and asked why she would do such a thing. She replied by telling him that she followed one who said, "Love your enemies."[20] Now in spite of how grand her act of forgiveness seems to us, it does not approach the forgiveness of God. Indeed, in order for her forgiveness to replicate that of God's divine forgiveness, she would have to marry the soldier and take him as her beloved as God is always willing to take us as his beloved.

Human beings are simply not capable of imagining such forgiveness. We are easily offended, and although we may be able to forgive an offense or two, if we were aware of much more, we would quickly reach the limit of how much we are willing to suffer to restore a relationship. Imagine if we were aware of every time a spouse or friend had an unkind thought about us. The only

20. Matthew 5:44.

people we would be able to maintain relationships with would be those we don't know well and with whom we spend little time.

Of course, God is aware of our every wayward thought—aware of every time we would rather focus our attention on some object of lust,[21] anger,[22] or worry[23] rather than his divine presence. He knows our deepest sins and responds to them with mercy. That is difficult to imagine. It is much easier to imagine a God who would torture Jesus rather than a God who would pray for his torturers to be forgiven. We are simply more comfortable with torture than with forgiveness. We are uncomfortable with the divine level of consciousness that we would have to ascend to in order to prefer a forgiving God to a torturing god. We want a god who is like us: a just god and not a merciful God because we prefer to relate to others through justice rather than through mercy and forgiveness.

This is part of the prejudicial understanding we bring to our reading of the Gospel. We emphasize those aspects of the Gospel that our understanding finds appealing, and we suppress those aspects that we find unappealing. We want to be like Jesus and have the power of the Holy Spirit flow through us as it flowed through him. We would love to be able to work miracles as he did, but we have little interest in praying for our torturers to be forgiven.[24] To suffer injustice for the sake of restoring relationship with the guilty is not very appealing. There is something upsetting about the innocent paying for the offense of the guilty. It certainly

21. Matthew 5:28.
22. Matthew 5:22.
23. Matthew 6:34.
24. Luke 23:34.

seems unfair that the guilty are free from the consequences of what they have done and can enjoy their relationship with the innocent as if the offense never took place, while the innocent must suffer the pain of the offense. No one likes pain, but the fact that it is the result of injustice makes it especially difficult to bear. Few of us respond to injustice and evil as Jesus did, but that is the great revelation of the Cross: Jesus showing us who God is and how he responds to evil. This is a God whose mercy is far more than we can fathom. We much prefer to see Jesus as a man suffering God's wrath in our place. Of course, Jesus is a man and the Cross is a dual revelation of both who God is and who we are. But the revelation of Jesus' humanity is not one of suffering God's wrath, but one of feeling abandoned by God only to wake up alive in the tomb. It is the revelation that we all experience when there is one set of footprints and we can no longer sense God's presence. Jesus did have to die, as we all have to die, but he reveals the good news that when we go through that darkest hour where we feel abandoned by God, we wake up alive in the tomb.

We almost all begin with a rather primitive concept of God as one who rewards some and punishes others based upon our varying prejudices. That is why the popular atonement theory is to see Jesus as our scapegoat: Our sin is placed upon him and we bear it no more. We may need to begin there, but that leaves us with a God that loves us very conditionally. This is a God who will pour forth his wrath upon us just as he did on Jesus if we do not meet the conditions he sets forth. That is where we usually begin, but the deeper understanding is that our need for a scapegoat is only to satisfy a need within *us*. God does not need a scapegoat in order to love us. It is we who need a scapegoat in order to approach what we initially believe to be a wrathful God. Scapegoating is never healthy, and it keeps us from the experience of God loving us in the midst of our sin. That is the great revelation of the Cross: a tortured God loving his torturers and praying for their forgiveness.

Jesus is willing to be our scapegoat. We may need a scapegoat because we can't imagine the depth of God's love, forgiveness, and mercy, but the idea of the scapegoat keeps us from seeing who we really are and who God really is. We like to blame our imperfections on others, but that prevents us from seeing our true selves. More importantly, it keeps us from seeing who God really is. Scapegoating gives us a picture of a God whose love is limited by what he finds in the objects of his affection. Such a view is to imagine that God must be like us and his love diminishes when imperfections appear within those he loves. We divorce our spouses and disown our children when we discover their imperfection—this is the nature of human love. We have little capacity to love the unlovely and almost no capacity to love our enemies. Our only hope of ever becoming like God in terms of love is to continually see our sinful state and experience God's love in the midst of that state. The constant experience of God's forgiveness and mercy is the only thing capable of making us into the kinds of creatures that can love as God loves. This is at the heart of the Jesus message but it is simply too divine for us, so we make it into religions that accommodate our human prejudices.

CHAPTER THREE

Jesus on Justice

WESTERN JUSTICE and God's mercy are antithetical and thus we must choose. Early in life most choose justice—at least the winners do. But hopefully, later in life, we all realize that no one is ultimately a winner—no one does it right—and we should all seek mercy. Sadly, some never realize this. Some are committed to the notion that "good" behavior should be rewarded and bad behavior punished. There was a girl who got pregnant at a Christian college. It was unexpected and the girl was devastated. Her friends in her dorm put together a basket of cute little gifts and notes of encouragement. Another student, however, could not understand why the pregnant girl was being rewarded for the wrong behavior that put her in that situation. This type of reaction can be traced back to our earliest and most consistent conditioning. Reward and punishment mold the basis for our interaction with family, friends, and even strangers. It is so much a part of our human world that we imagine it must be a part of God's world, as well. Our initial concept of God is almost always a just god who rewards goodness and punishes evil. This is the god we first encounter and the god we will insist upon, unless we take seriously the things that Jesus says.

Christians are often heard to profess that God is both merciful and just, and you will remember from the last chapter that a dominant atonement theory has God pouring forth his wrath upon Jesus to satisfy some strange sense of justice where the innocent pays for the sins of the guilty. But, it could be asked, how is that justice rather than forgiveness? In fact, the innocent paying for the sins of the guilty is the greatest of all injustices, but it is exactly what forgiveness is. The Cross is a horrible picture of justice, but a beautiful picture of mercy and forgiveness.

We insist, however, upon a God who is just and not simply merciful. Mercy alone is too much for us. We insist that a perfect God would not allow anyone to escape his justice, as people often escape the justice of human authority. The problem with this is that if we take the Gospel seriously, no one meets God's standard of righteousness. None of us love our enemies and pray for our torturers the way Jesus did.[25] Nor do we dwell in a constant awareness of God's presence the way Jesus did. Of course, most Christians don't use Jesus as their standard for righteousness. They make Jesus into God in order that they don't have to live by the divine standard that he sets forth. Their standard for righteousness is a human standard: a standard that judges behavior and not the heart. When we judge human beings according to their behavior some people appear much better than others, but Jesus tells us that God judges the heart and when he does we all come up lacking.

None of us have our hearts set upon God and an awareness of his presence the way Jesus did. Certainly, there may be times when we do achieve an awareness of the Divine presence but we cannot maintain that very long. Our hearts are prone to wander and the distractions of the world capture our attention and keep

25. Luke 23:34.

us from an awareness of the Divine presence and the fullness of life that comes with that awareness. This is the righteousness that Jesus sets forth in the Gospels but we all fall short of that divine standard. This standard should motivate us to seek mercy rather than justice.

Justice is a necessary part of our human world, and at times we may feel virtuous for having acted justly, but we should never lose sight of the fact that it is a *human* virtue rather than a divine virtue. The ancient Greeks thought it was a cardinal virtue along with courage, temperance, and wisdom. But human virtues are not necessarily divine virtues. Jesus says, "You are those who justify yourselves in the sight of others; but God knows your hearts; for what is prized by human beings is an abomination in the sight of God."[26] Indeed, we love justice because it gives us a feeling of righteousness when we see the sins of others. We want other's bad behavior punished and our good behavior rewarded. Our prejudice toward justice is part of our human condition, and within the human realm justice does appear to be a virtue, but Jesus tells us that we all enter into the Divine presence through mercy and never through our achieving righteousness in God's sight. This is the narrow gate[27] of which Jesus speaks, but what keeps us from that narrow gate is our prejudice toward justice.

The virtue of justice is based upon the idea of what is my own and what is not my own. When we respect what is our own and do not claim for ourselves what is not our own we are deemed just. But Jesus tells us that nothing is our own. In the divine rather than human realm everything is God's and nothing is our own. In

26. Luke 16:15.
27. Matthew 7:13-14.

David Hume's, *An Enquiry Concerning the Principles of Morals*, he says that in a heavenly state every virtue would flourish except justice and respect for what is our own.

> It seems evident, that, in such a happy state, every other social virtue would flourish, and receive tenfold increase; but the cautious, jealous virtue of justice, would never once have been dreamt of. For what purpose make a partition of goods, where everyone has already more than enough?[28]

Hume points out that in both circumstances of great abundance and of great privation, property rights are non-existent. When there is great abundance, if someone should take the apple from my hand, I simply pick another. Likewise, when there is great scarcity, the fact that the apple is in my hand does not stop another from taking it from me in order to survive. It is only in this middle realm between heaven and hell where justice is a virtue. Even Aristotle knew that when human beings function on that higher plain, there is no need for justice. He says, "When men are friends, they have no need of justice at all."[29]

Of course, justice is a concept that applies not only to property and possessions but also to human behavior and our reaction to it. Our human experience has conditioned us to believe that good behavior deserves to be rewarded and bad behavior punished. We applaud both, and when bad behavior goes unpunished, or good behavior goes unrewarded, we think it unjust. We believe

---

28. Hume, David. *An Inquiry concerning the Principles of Morals*. Ed. Ralph Cohen. *The Essential Works of David Hume*. New York: Bantam Books, 1965, p. 190.

29. Aristotle. *Nicomachean Ethics*. VIII. 1. 27.

that our behavior is something we own and we deserve merit when it is good and sanction when it is bad. Most often, however, our behavior is more the product of our conditioning rather than something for which we deserve praise or blame. Some have had great advantages and others great disadvantages and, perhaps for that reason, Jesus' teachings run contrary to our prejudice toward justice.

> "For the kingdom of heaven is like a landowner who went out early in the morning to hire laborers for his vineyard. After agreeing with the laborers for the usual daily wage, he sent them into his vineyard. When he went out about nine o'clock, he saw others standing idle in the marketplace; and he said to them, 'You also go into the vineyard, and I will pay you whatever is right.' So they went. When he went out again about noon and about three o'clock, he did the same. And about five o'clock he went out and found others standing around; and he said to them, 'Why are you standing here idle all day?' They said to him, 'Because no one has hired us.' He said to them, 'You also go into the vineyard.' When evening came, the owner of the vineyard said to his manager, 'Call the laborers and give them their pay, beginning with the last and then going to the first.' When those hired about five o'clock came, each of them received the usual daily wage. Now when the first came, they thought they would receive more; but each of them also received the usual daily wage. And when they received it, they grumbled against the landowner, saying, 'These last worked only one hour, and you have made them equal to us who have borne the burden of the day and the scorching heat.' But he replied to one of them, 'Friend, I am doing you no wrong; did you not agree with me for the

> usual daily wage? Take what belongs to you and go; I choose to give to this last the same as I give to you. Am I not allowed to do what I choose with what belongs to me? Or are you envious because I am generous? So the last will be first, and the first will be last."[30]

Most Americans hate this teaching of Jesus. We want a god who is just and rewards us in proportion to our goodness. Those who labored all day did more good than those who labored only one hour, and we think they are right for wanting to be compensated accordingly. We despise generosity when it is extended to those we deem less worthy. Listen to all those religious people today who constantly complain about the welfare cheats who don't deserve the handout because they haven't worked for it. Our idea of justice is such a deep human prejudice and so much a part of our human world, we can't hear Jesus when he speaks about mercy and against justice. Jesus ends the parable above by saying, "The last will be first, and the first will be last."[31]

He is making grateful the undeserving, and making resentful those who see themselves as deserving. When we read this parable, do we side with the resentful or the grateful? That should inform us to a great extent as to where we are with Jesus. Do we love God's generosity and mercy or do we resent it? Are we the last who will be first or the first who will be last? People who see themselves as good, righteous people hate mercy and love justice. Those who love justice hate the landowner and those who love mercy love him. Likewise, there are two types of Christians: those

30. Matthew 20:1-16.
31. Matthew 20:16.

who love justice and those who love mercy. In this parable you can't have both. You have to choose which you love and which you hate. The winners love justice and hate mercy, but the losers love mercy.

Of course, the greatest example of Jesus coming out on the side of mercy rather than justice is the parable of the Prodigal Son.[32] There the one son does it right and that turns out to be bad, while the other son does it wrong and that turns out to be good. The good son turns out to be resentful because he doesn't appreciate his father's mercy. He wants his father to love him more than his brother because of his goodness, while the bad son becomes the recipient of mercy and therefore comes to know and love his father in a way that the good son never does. The story ends with the good son refusing to come to the party that is being given for the bad son. It is possible that some will choose Hell rather than Heaven when they see how merciful God really is.

Our world does not prepare us very well for Heaven. We live in a culture that rewards the *winners* and punishes the *losers*, but God's kingdom is a kingdom of losers. Thus, it is wise for each of us to recognize that we are losers in need of God's mercy, even though that is difficult for us to do. From our perspective, there is a vast difference among human beings in terms of goodness and evil, but that is because we judge behavior rather than the heart. God, on the other hand, judges the heart and, when he does, he finds that none are good and all are in need of mercy.

Several years ago, a student gave his professor a memorable lesson on this topic while they were reading Plato's *Republic*. At

32. Luke 15:11-32.

the beginning of book two, Glaucon challenges Socrates, and his idea of justice, with a myth concerning the ancestor of Gyges, the Lydian. In the myth, Gyges' ancestor was a shepherd who one day after a great deluge and earthquake noticed a chasm where he was shepherding. Upon entering the chasm he found a great hollow bronze horse which contained a corpse. The corpse had nothing on but a gold ring which Gyges' ancestor took before returning to the outer world. In wearing the ring, he noticed that when he turned the collet or face of the ring in toward his palm, he became invisible. Upon turning the ring the other way, he would reappear. With the ability to become invisible at will, the shepherd had acquired the power to do injustice and not suffer for it. With this power, he chose to seduce the king's wife and kill the king in order to take his kingdom. Although his ability to become invisible would seem a hindrance in his seduction of the queen, it would allow him to escape from suffering for having done injustice if his plan went awry.

The story is meant to illustrate that if someone had the power to do injustice and not suffer for it they would always do injustice. Glaucon says to Socrates that if there were two rings and one was given to the just man and one to the unjust man, they would both do injustice. Socrates spends the next nine books of the *Republic* trying to convince his interlocutors that even if you could do injustice and never suffer for it, it would still be in your interest to act justly. Once the class was over, the above-mentioned student approached the professor and said something that the professor found surprising at first. What he said was, "Don't we all have a ring of Gyges?" The professor looked at him curiously. The student's response: "It's our imagination."

What a significant insight. Knowing this story can be helpful in knowing the Jesus message on a deeper level. Over the years, that has helped me see just how deep this Jesus thing goes. It is true that, as long as evil remains in our heads and hearts we can do all manner of evil without suffering for such injustice. We may behave justly, for fear of being punished or thought badly of, but we can do evil with impunity if we restrict it to our imagination. From our human perspective that seems innocuous since we think no one is harmed by imagined injustice. Of course, although others might not be harmed by such thoughts and feelings they do harm to those who bear them and are what separate us from an awareness of God's presence. Jesus is not interested in morality as we understand it: he tells us of the deeper sins within our hearts and minds.

> "You have heard that it was said to those of ancient times, 'You shall not commit murder'; and 'whoever murders shall be liable to judgment.' But I say to you that if you are angry with a brother or sister, you are liable to judgment."[33]

A little later he says the same thing about adultery.

> "You have heard that it was said, 'You shall not commit adultery.' But I say to you that everyone who looks at a woman with lust has already committed adultery with her in his heart."[34]

Jesus is always pointing to our real sin or our real offense against God; that is, that God is not in all of our thoughts. He tells

33. Matthew 5:21-22.
34. Matthew 5:27-28.

us, "You shall love the Lord your God with all your heart, and with all your soul, and with all your mind. This is the greatest and first commandment."[35] To love in this way requires that we are attentive to God in all that we do, as Jesus was always attentive to the Divine presence that he referred to as his Father. Most of us fail miserably at this and are distracted by all the things Jesus talks about in the Sermon on the Mount and elsewhere throughout the Gospels. Some religious zealots have fared slightly better by trying to cleanse their hearts and minds by living an ascetic life free from such distractions, but that misses the point. The point is not to become righteous by avoiding such thoughts, but rather to see such thoughts as the opportunity for repentance and the experience of God's mercy. This is the central theme of the Gospel: that righteousness is out of our reach and it was never God's intention that we become righteous. Of course, we are constantly told to strive after righteousness, but when we see what real righteousness is all about as Jesus reveals it, we see that we all fail, and, in recognizing our failure come to repentance and the experience of God's mercy.

We were created in order to love God and therein become like him, but loving God is not something that we *do* but something that is given to us. It is produced in us through the experience of God's unconditional love which comes through his mercy. "We cannot really trust that we are loved until we know that we are loved even with our faults. …unconditional love is hard to understand and that, once grasped, it changes whatever else you thought you understood."[36] Unfortunately, although it changes us,

---

35. Matthew 22:37-38.

36. T. M. Luhrmann. *When God Talks Back*. Alfred A. Knopf, 2012. 325.

it does so only for the moment. We quickly forget the experience of mercy and slip back into our much more comfortable pursuit of righteousness. To become merciful, we must constantly experience being the recipients of mercy through repentance. That alone makes us merciful and any other way is mere pretense to mercy. We may act as if we were merciful but to have mercy deep down in our soul we must receive much mercy. The right religious belief will never make us merciful. Mercy has to be experienced and experienced repeatedly. Sadly, most Christian denominations are founded upon theologies that point us toward righteousness rather than mercy. Thus, our theologies preserve our idea of justice as some people being rewarded for their beliefs and rituals and others punished for not having the right theology. We want a just God who determines heaven or hell based upon our righteousness and not his mercy and generosity.

One of the biggest choices in life is our choice between mercy and justice. We want both and insist that God is both merciful and just, but in fact it is *we* who want to be both. Justice comes easily to us. We are much more comfortable with it than we are with mercy. Mercy is simply too divine for us. It is a higher level of consciousness, and we need to experience it repeatedly in order for it to take root within us and cause us to ascend to that more divine level of consciousness. There is a judge who wanted the Ten Commandments posted in his courtroom. We can easily imagine that kind of justice, but we cannot imagine a judge who would post the Sermon on the Mount. Using such guidelines would result in everyone being guilty and in need of mercy, and that is simply too divine for this world.

Before leaving this chapter it should be mentioned that there is an alternative notion of justice that Jesus does not oppose. This alternative notion of justice is greatly overshadowed by the dominant notion of justice that prevails, especially in this country. That notion is essentially about establishing and protecting what is our own, and Jesus exposes that idea of justice for the illusion it is. There is, however, another notion of justice that is about establishing and protecting what is owed to the marginalized and least privileged of God's children. This is the notion of justice that Jesus consistently endorses. Those that have much love the dominant notion of justice because it protects what they consider their own, but there is a divine justice that centers on what is owed to those that have nothing. Justice that seeks to protect what we consider our own is established by human authority, while justice that focuses on what is owed to what Jesus calls "the least of these my brethren" is established by divine authority. Another name for this less dominant notion of justice is mercy.

CHAPTER FOUR

Jesus on Wealth

LIKE RELIGION AND JUSTICE, wealth is another thing we value, and which many even believe is a reward for righteousness. Indeed, the sociologist Max Weber (1864-1920) argued that Marx was wrong about the origins of capitalism and, in fact, capitalism developed out of the Protestant work ethic. At the heart of the Protestant work ethic was the idea that hard work and not indulging in earthly pleasures was the formula for successful Christian living. Of course if someone works hard and is not spending his or her money on earthly pleasure, surplus or capital starts to accumulate. Such surplus was not simply a sign that someone was rich but that they were righteous and living a good, Christian life.

Jesus, however, has more to say against wealth than perhaps anything else other than hypocrisy and the pretense to righteousness. Like Marx, Jesus saw wealth as a great evil. The reason Marx saw wealth as evil was primarily because of the effect it had on others who were forced to live in poverty because of the few who possessed all of the resources. Marx thought that people would eventually see that their economic woes were caused by the rich and would eventually do something about it. Others, like Adam Smith (1723-1790) and Thorsten Veblen (1857-1920) recognized there was an admiration for the rich among the poor that might never go away. Jesus, however, doesn't address the problem of wealth from the perspective of its effect upon the poor but rather its effect upon the rich. According to Jesus, wealth, and the identity it produces, destroys the souls of those who succumb to its allure. In the parable of the Rich Man and Lazarus, Jesus says,

> "There was a rich man who was dressed in purple and fine linen and who feasted sumptuously every day. And at his gate lay a poor man named Lazarus, covered with sores, who longed to satisfy his hunger with what fell from the rich man's table; even the dogs would come and lick his sores. The poor man died and was carried away by the angels to be with Abraham. The rich man also died and was buried. In Hades, where he was being tormented, he looked up and saw Abraham far away with Lazarus by his side. He called out 'Father Abraham, have mercy on me, and send Lazarus to dip the tip of his finger in water and cool my tongue; for I am in agony in these flames.' But Abraham said, 'Child, remember that during your lifetime you received your good things, and Lazarus in like manner evil things; but now he is comforted here, and you are in agony. Besides all this, between you and us a great chasm has been fixed, so that those who might want to pass from here to you cannot do so, and no one can cross from there to us.' "[37]

In this parable, it is not clear why this rich man is in torment, nor does Jesus say that God is the one tormenting him. What Jesus does tell us is that the man was rich and lived well when he was alive. So is the point of the parable that riches are the cause of

37. Luke 16:19-26.

his torment? That is certainly not the perspective of most television ministries that tell us that wealth and economic prosperity are the result of following Jesus. According to their reading of the Gospel, God blesses us with wealth, but Jesus' teachings are always *against* wealth. This should further convince us that our religious beliefs are much more about our prejudices and what we want to see rather than Jesus saying in Luke's Gospel,

> "Do not store up for yourselves treasures on earth, where moth and rust consume and where thieves break in and steal; but store up for yourselves treasures in heaven, where neither moth nor rust consumes and where thieves do not break in and steal. For where your treasure is, there your heart will be also."[38]

Many Christians will argue that they are storing up treasure in heaven but God is also blessing them with wealth here as well. But what do such Christians do with Jesus saying in Luke's Gospel, "Woe to you who are rich, for you have received your consolation."[39] Likewise, in the parable of the Sower and the Seed, which appears in all three of the Synoptic Gospels, Jesus tells us that the seed that "was sown among thorns, this is the one who hears the word, but the cares of the world and the lure of *wealth* [my emphasis] choke the word, and it yields nothing."[40] Jesus also tells us in the Synoptic Gospels, "It is easier for a camel to go through the eye of a needle than for someone who is rich to

38. Matthew 6:19-21.
39. Luke 6:24.
40. Matthew 13:22; also see Mark 4:19; Luke 8:14.

enter the kingdom of God,"[41] and in Luke's Gospel, he presents us with a parable about a man who sought wealth rather than God.

> "The land of a rich man produced abundantly. And he thought to himself, 'What should I do, for I have no place to store my crops?' Then he said, 'I will do this: I will pull down my barns and build larger ones, and there I will store all my grain and my goods. And I will say to my soul, Soul, you have ample goods laid up for many years; relax, eat, drink, be merry.' But God said to him, 'You fool! This very night your life is being demanded of you. And the things you have prepared, whose will they be?' So it is with those who store up treasures for themselves but are not rich toward God."[42]

Jesus' point is that we can find security and rest in God alone, and to try to find it anywhere else is both idolatrous and foolish. Jesus also points out the idolatrous nature of wealth when he tells us that we cannot serve two masters. He says very specifically that the two masters are God and wealth.

> "No one can serve two masters; for a slave will either hate the one and love the other, or be devoted to the one and despise the other. You cannot serve God and wealth."[43]

Jesus' teachings against sexual immorality do not compare with his teachings against wealth. Strangely, many churches will not extend membership to homosexuals, but rich people are welcome in spite of all of Jesus' teachings. Of course, that is easy

41. Matthew 19:24; also see Mark 10:23-25; Luke 18:24.
42. Luke 12:16-21.
43. Matthew 6:24; also see Luke 16:13.

enough to understand. Our prejudice toward wealth makes it impossible to hear Jesus' teachings on this matter. In fact, if we hear Christians defend the idea of wealth they never reference Jesus, but instead quote Paul and argue that it is the *love* of money that is evil, and therefore not money itself.[44] There may be some truth to this since poor people can love wealth and lust after it even in its absence. The poor can worship money, just as the powerless can lust after power, and the nobodies can dream of being somebody. Such things can still be the idols we worship even when we have no access to them. But when people quote Paul rather than Jesus on wealth, their intention is clear. They want to argue that it is not money itself but the "love" of money that is the issue. If it is the love of money rather than money itself, they can argue that they may have wealth but they really don't "love" it. Even if that were true, however, and we could convince ourselves that we don't love money, it is not so easy to convince ourselves that we are not identified by it.

Economists tell us that money has three functions: a means of exchange, a store of value (capital), and a measure of value. In our capitalist culture money is the means by which we measure value. Just as we measure distance in miles, and temperature in degrees, we measure value in terms of money. How good is that suit or car? The monetary price tells us its worth. In many people's minds, a person's wealth tells us the worth of that person. This is the illusion Jesus addresses; that is, that a person's value and source of identity is based on money, that a person is important and of greater value than others because of money.

44. 1 Timothy 6:10.

In our modern world, however, there is another source of personal value in addition to that of money. Today, fame also gives the false impression that some people are of greater value than others. Of course, Jesus never addresses the matter of fame. Celebrities did not exist in the ancient world, and fame was something reserved for royalty. Private people had no means by which they could become famous. Fame or celebrity is the idea that a person is known by a great number of people who have no personal contact with that individual. It has been said that Martin Luther was the first non-royal celebrity in the history of the world. Luther was born a half century after the invention of the printing press and, before the printing press became sophisticated enough to print books, it produced short tracts, which was exactly what Luther was writing. There were literally millions of these short Lutheran tracts all over Europe and everyone knew the name, Martin Luther. Today, celebrity is a common notion and part of the world we inherit, but it, like money, can be a terrible affliction for those who acquire it. It gives them the illusion that, because they are identified by a great many people, they themselves are greater than the rest of us whose identity is established by the handsful of people that make up our social world.

Certainly there is a difference between wealth and celebrity. Some celebrities are not wealthy and some wealthy people are not celebrities. Aristotle Onassis had a theory about celebrity. He was one of the richest men in the world, but no one knew who he was until he became the major stockholder in the company that controlled the casino at Monte Carlo. He later theorized that one becomes a celebrity by controlling the way people spend their leisure time. Our celebrities are movies stars, sports figures, authors, even restaurateurs if their restaurant is not just a place to eat but a place to spend leisure time. As with wealth, the idea of celebrity creates the illusion that, because the famous individual is identifiable by a great multitude of people, their identity is more substantial than ours. Of course, a healthy identity, or sense of who we really are, should come from those who know us best and not great multitudes of people who know very little about us. As with money, however, celebrity provides us with a false identity, creating the illusion that we are much more attractive or fascinating than we really are. The majority of us would like to be celebrities; being famous provides one with an identity which appears more meaningful than that of ordinary people and gives that person a place and authority above others. Consequently, baseball players tell us what coffee to drink and movie stars what credit card to use. How strange! It is, however, more than simply *strange* when celebrities are the ones we look to in order to understand how to follow Jesus. At a recent local prayer breakfast, the guest speaker was a movie star who two years previously had had a conversion experience. He was chosen because many people would be interested in his testimony, not because of his saintliness, but because of his celebrity. The words of television preachers are given more credence simply because they are on television and therefore known to a great many people. Such preachers command authority, not by what they say, but by their celebrity.

It is hard to hear Jesus on this matter since the rich and famous are the major interpreters of the Gospel today. The rich buy television and radio stations to project their ideas on how to read the Gospel, and celebrities rather than saints write the majority of books. Go to any bookstore and you will see it is celebrities who author the books that purport to instruct us in the Christian life. Publishers know that, in order to sell large quantities of books, the author has to be identifiable by a great many people. Consequently, television preachers, sports stars, and every other imaginable celebrity are the ones from whom we are given spiritual direction. Sadly, their spiritual authority comes from their celebrity rather than their saintliness.

As with wealth, the idea of celebrity is not only detrimental in the way it affects others, but it is especially detrimental to the individual who bears the mantle of celebrity. As we have said, the celebrity's identity may seem greater than the average person since it is shaped by great masses of people while the rest of us have our sense of ourselves shaped only by the handsful of people who make up our social world. Of course, this is obviously an illusion since the masses that establish the celebrity's identity really don't know that person at all. In order to have a healthy identity it must be formed by people who really do know who we are. Unfortunately, even our closest friends don't really know us, and that is why Francis Assisi is reported to have said, "I am who God says I am, no more and no less." That certainly is the picture of identity that Jesus is presenting and calling us to seek. God is the only one who truly knows us and is capable of giving us an identity that is more than an illusion, but our cultural prejudice on this matter is enormously strong. We admire identities formed out of wealth and celebrity. Such identities may be illusions, but they are part of the cultural prejudices we inherit and they keep us from hearing Jesus on this matter.

Interestingly, the saint's identity is the very opposite of that of the rich and famous. The masses tell the rich and famous they are great but Jesus tells us we are all prodigals in need of mercy. If we can bear the shock to our egos, the identity that the saint finds in God alone is infinitely more substantial than an identity provided by wealth or fame. It is very hard to establish such an identity in God, however, since our prejudices toward wealth and fame constantly pull us in the opposite direction. If we don't experience God's unconditional love, we will seek love and affirmation from whatever sources we can find, and the more sources the better. But if we are really honest, we know that what others love about us is the illusion we present. The only true and healthy source of identity comes from one who knows every wicked and unkind thought we have ever had and still loves us. No human being is capable of knowing all of our deepest thoughts, and no human being is capable of loving us in spite of such knowledge. Our ultimate sense of identity has to come from God and God alone. This is what the saint understands: we are who God says we are, no more and no less.

We all suffer from the same illusion. We may not have what the rich and famous have but, like them, we want to be identified by others who don't really know us. We want to be judged by our external behavior and the superficial image we present. Jesus' teachings, however, are aimed at discrediting that image. This is what the real saint understands. As a consequence, they are more repentant and much more the recipient of God's mercy than the rest of us. It is not that they are immune to the identity others create for them out of the good they see in them, but they know it for the lie it is and turn away from it over and over again. They see wealth and fame for the cultural prejudices they are, and they are not deluded by them, but live in a constant state of repentance because of them.

Instead of ascending to wealth and fame, the saint's journey is one of descent. In contrast to the ladder of success that our culture tells us we should climb, the saint's journey is a downward journey through repentance and the experience of God's mercy. Indeed, we enter heaven as we descend into the littleness of the child whose identity is founded in nothing more than his or her parents' love. This was our identity as we entered the world, and it will be our identity as we exit the world as well. The saints, however, wish to live in that state throughout their earthly existence, despite the fact that it is nearly impossible to do so. The world constantly imposes a very different identity upon us, and whether it tells us we are celebrities or *nobodies*, it is always presenting us with an identity which, albeit false, seems to be confirmed by others. Thus, the saint is in the difficult position of having to constantly repent or turn away from that false identity and back to an identity to be found in God alone. Such a turn back toward God is especially difficult for the rich and famous, since they are made aware by everyone, except Jesus, that their identity is significant and should be embraced rather than abandoned. Jesus, however, is constantly warning us of the cultural prejudices that keep us from the fullness of life God has for us.

CHAPTER FIVE

Jesus on Family

CHRISTIANITY, PARTICULARLY as it is currently practiced in the United States, is the great defender of the family and traditional family values. But Jesus never has anything positive to say about the family. In fact all his teachings about the family are negative, and yet most who consider themselves his followers turn a proverbial blind eye to them. In all three of the synoptic Gospels, we see Jesus being told that his mother and brothers and sisters are outside and wish to see him, but his response is quite startling.

> A crowd was sitting around him; and they said to him, "Your mother and your brothers and sisters are outside, asking for you." And he replied, "Who are my mother and my brothers?" And looking at those who sat around him, he said, "Here are my mother and my brothers! Whoever does the will of God is my brother and sister and mother."[45]

In another place he tells us that he came to divide families.

> "For I have come to set a man against his father, and a daughter against her mother, and a daughter-in-law against her

45. Mark 3:31-35;. also see Matthew 12:47; Luke 8:20.

> mother-in-law; and one's foes will be members of one's own household."[46]

Or as he says in Luke's Gospel:

> "Do you think that I came to bring peace to the earth? No, I tell you, but rather division! From now on five in one household will be divided, three against two, and two against three; they will be divided: father against son and son against father, mother against daughter and daughter against mother, mother-in-law against daughter-in-law and daughter-in-law against mother-in-law."[47]

The division that Jesus is talking about here is certainly interpreted in different ways. Most interpretations center on doctrinal differences between Christian denominations and what are the essential factors that make someone a Christian but these matters have little to do with the actual teaching of Jesus.[48] I think the conflict Jesus has in mind is rather the conflict between those who see how radical the Jesus message is and begin to take on the mind of Christ, and those content with the understanding they inherit from their culture and language community. The latter want a Jesus who will conform to their prejudices rather than one who will destroy those prejudices.

All Christians claim they want Jesus, but the question is: how much of Jesus are you willing to embrace? How much of your

46. Matthew 10:35-36.

47. Luke 12:51-53.

48. I have often heard of conflicts within families over the importance of things like Baptism, the Born Again experience, or whether someone is a Protestant or Catholic.

sacred understanding are you willing to let him destroy in order to come to the more divine perspective or level of consciousness he offers us in the Gospels? In order to take on this perspective, we must see that there is something wrong with our inherited perspective. Everyone wants Jesus the Savior who assures us of heaven, but the Jesus who does violence to our sacred prejudices is another matter. A little of Jesus is nice, but the radical Jesus who threatens to overthrow the way we interpret nearly everything is another matter. The mind of Christ is simply too radical for us. I recently heard a devout Christian say, "I love the Bible, but that 'love your enemies' stuff is a bit much." Jesus is simply too much for us, and that is what should keep us in an almost-constant state of repentance and the experience of God's mercy.

Of course, the most radical and shocking thing Jesus ever said about the family is found in Luke's Gospel where he says,

> "If anyone comes to me and does not hate his own father and mother and wife and children and brothers and sisters, yes, and even his own life, he cannot be my disciple."[49]

Most Christians don't know what to do with this, so they simply ignore it. When forced to deal with it, they usually argue that Jesus really doesn't mean that we are to "hate" our families and our lives, but that we are to love God so much more that all earthly affection would look like hate. Even that is quite radical, but the more radical reading is that *nothing is our own* and to love what we consider our own is the source of much of the evil in the world. Jesus calls us to love our enemies,[50] and we can do that to

49. Luke 14:26.ESV
50. Matthew 5:44.

a limited extent, or until someone does harm to *my* wife, *my* children, *my* mother, or *my* country. That calls for a violent response because they have done evil to what is *mine*. The divine point that Jesus is making here, and what is so evil about loving our own, is that nothing is really our own—everything is God's. Jesus' divine perspective sees this in a way that we cannot, since our human prejudice believes there are things that are mine and no one else's, and I have a right to defend what is my own and punish those who violate what is *mine*.

Some are in a better position to receive Jesus' divine perspective because their human prejudice has been destroyed. A case in point is a particular man who was raised without a father. When Dan was a child, he had a friend whose father was very active in his son's life, and he always extended kindness to Dan by including him in whatever activities he was doing with his son. That sounds commendable, and by human standards the father was certainly good to do that. Dan, however, said that, as nice as the man was, he always knew that the man preferred his own son to him. He went on to say that he always thought there was something evil about that, and the only way it wouldn't be evil is if there was a father who loved everyone the same. No one but the fatherless can see the evil in loving our own. That is why Jesus is always praising the marginalized, since they are without many of our common, human prejudices that keep us from the divine perspective Jesus is offering. Those who have what we call "loving fathers," would think it terrible if their father loved the stranger as much as the son, but that keeps us from seeing who God is. God is the father of everyone and there is no distinction in terms of his fatherhood.

In *Have a Little Faith,* Mitch Albom relates a story of being in Hebrew class as a child and reading about Moses crossing the Red Sea.

> After the Israelites safely crossed the Red Sea, the Egyptians chased after them and were drowned. God's angels wanted to celebrate the enemy's demise. According to the commentary, God saw this and grew angry. He said in essence: "Stop celebrating. For those were my children too."[51]

Our human prejudice tells us that it is good to love one's own, but certainly there is nothing virtuous or praiseworthy in that. Even the most despicable of people love what is their own, simply because it is theirs. There is a George MacDonald book in which the author tells a story about an evil man who was sadly lacking in any redeeming qualities. At one point in describing him, MacDonald says that he *did* love his children, but only because they were his.[52] Jesus' perspective is very different. Jesus knows that everything is God's and nothing is our own. Jesus knew that his life was not his own, and this is why he tells us that we have to lose our lives, or our ownership of it, in order to find life in God.[53] God loves us simply because we are his creation, and God loves all of his creation.

One could argue that we do have God's perspective because we love our children as our creation, just as God loves his creation. But that is the lie. Our children are not our creation but God's. It is not surprising that this lie is seldom questioned. Our lives are built around storing up what is our own and protecting it from

---

51. Mitch Albom. *Have a Little Faith.* New York: Hyperion, 2009. 76.
52. George McDonald, *The Maiden's Bequest,* Bethany House, 1985.
53. John 12:25; Matthew 10:39.

others. Our human prejudice is that the value of a person is measured by how much is his or her own, be it children, houses, fame, or wealth. This is why some have quipped that "Christianity is a great idea; too bad no one has ever tried it," or that "Jesus was the only Christian." Of course, Jesus was not a Christian but someone who had such a deep intimacy with the Divine that he knew things about God that our deep human prejudices keep us from seeing. Furthermore, because we remain committed to the deep prejudices through which we interpret and make sense of our lives, we cannot hear the words of the one we claim to worship as Divine.

> "You have heard it said, 'An eye for an eye and a tooth for a tooth.' But I say to you, do not resist an evildoer. But if anyone strikes you on the right check, turn the other also; and if anyone wants to sue you and take your coat, give your cloak as well."[54]

While it might appear that Jesus is calling us all to be ascetic monks, it seems doubtful that that is the message. Being an ascetic monk can easily produce pride rather than humility within us. It seems Jesus' hope is rather that we would see how far short we fall and therein realize our constant need for mercy. What humbles us is that we see that none are righteous. Jesus' life and teachings should convince us that righteousness is way beyond us and our relationship with God can only be sustained through God's mercy. Jesus wants us to be like him, not in terms of righteousness, but rather in terms of forgiveness and mercy.

Our theologies are formulas for becoming righteous or sinless in God's sight, but Jesus tells us he is only interested in sinners.

54. Matthew 5:38-40.

That is because Jesus knows that the only way to be right with God is through God's mercy and not our sinlessness. Theologies that promise to make us sinless miss the major thrust of Jesus' teachings. Our sin is much deeper than we imagine and we cannot escape it. It is a real part of who we are, and it is meant to bring us to repentance and the experience of God's mercy. We are all deeply flawed, but it is through these flaws that the light of God's mercy comes in. It is this mercy that is divine. Our preference is to see righteousness as sinlessness, but that is always a pretense by people who really don't know themselves. It is a vain attempt to appease a god who is too much like us: a god who only loves that which is good and beautiful. Mercy, however, is love for the unlovely. We don't marvel when we see people making a pretense to sinlessness, but we do marvel when we witness genuine forgiveness and mercy. Of course, a pretense to righteousness is painless and makes us feel good about ourselves, while forgiveness and mercy are all about suffering: either suffering an offense ourselves (forgiveness), or entering into the suffering of others (mercy).

Jesus' Copernican revolution is so counterintuitive. It is the narrow gate[55] that only the sinner finds, and so much of Jesus' teachings are trying to get us to see what sinners we are. Our love of family is just such an instance. Of course, it is difficult to imagine living without such natural affection for one's own, but we are not intended to live as such. Rather, Jesus is showing us another less than divine prejudice that keeps us from seeing who God really is. If we begin to see who God really is, our love of family

55. Matthew 7:13-14.

should produce contrition and the further experience of God's mercy. Even those who claim to be the most righteous would have to concede that they are sinners on this count. It is our failure to live as Jesus instructs that continually brings us to the experience of God's mercy, and it is that experience that begins to make us into his merciful likeness. So, when Jesus tells us to hate our families, he is not pointing us toward righteousness but toward repentance and the experience of mercy. Certainly love of family is essential to human society, especially where minor children are involved. It is even difficult to imagine what our human condition would be like without such natural affection, but it is human rather than divine affection.

From the divine perspective Jesus offers, nothing is our own; everything is God's. But God does not own us the way we wish to own our children, loved ones, and even ourselves. We wish to have power in order to take charge of our own lives and the lives of those around us. God never *owns* us the way drugs, alcohol, sex, or other human beings may own us. God grants complete freedom to his creation and never takes the reins; we must constantly give them to him through repentance, since in every hour of our lives we deceive ourselves into believing that we are competent to be the captains of our soul and find the happiness we seek. The truth, however, is that we are plagued by prejudices that tell us we can find happiness in our religions or families, and that life would be meaningful if we had enough wealth or if we were able to achieve justice. Jesus tells us that such idols are incapable of providing happiness, and are in fact the very things that should bring us to repentance and the experience of mercy.

CHAPTER SIX

Jesus on Faith

IN ADDITION TO Jesus' radical teachings against the sacred prejudices that most of us hold concerning religion, justice, wealth, and family, Jesus also has a concept of faith that is unique and very different from what we refer to as religious faith today. Our contemporary notion of religious faith generally entails a belief in a certain theological tradition; that is, it is about believing in a set of doctrines, practices, and ways of conceptualizing the Divine. That kind of faith has almost nothing to do with the kind of faith Jesus is talking about.

When Jesus speaks of faith it is something that comes out of personal experience and not some inherited theological understanding. How strange that many people who claim to have a personal relationship with Jesus have a theology which they hold to be immutable and certain. That seems to undermine the idea of a personal relationship, since in a personal relationship our understanding of the other person is always changing with our additional experiences of them. If we are in a relationship with a person and our understanding of them hasn't changed in thirty years, then it seems apparent that we never really had a personal relationship, because in such a connection we would have come to know them on an ever-deeper level.

Of course, the Gospels also present faith as a belief in an inherited religious tradition but that is the faith of the religious leaders who opposed Jesus at every turn. That is also the kind of faith with which we almost all begin, and some retain that faith all of their lives. That is easy to do, since the major interpreters of Jesus' message have been people with faith in a religious tradition, but what Jesus praises as great faith is much bigger than any religious tradition. In the only two instances where Jesus says that someone has great faith, neither person is of the same religious tradition as Jesus. In the one instance, a Canaanite woman comes to Jesus asking for mercy concerning her daughter who is severely possessed by a demon.

> And behold, a Canaanite woman from that region came out and cried, "Have mercy on me, O Lord, Son of David; my daughter is severely possessed by a demon." But he did not answer her a word. And his disciples came and begged him, saying, "Send her away, for she is crying after us." He answered, "I was sent only to the lost sheep of the house of Israel." But she came and knelt before him, saying, "Lord, help me." And he answered, "It is not fair to take the children's bread and throw it to the dogs." She said, "Yes, Lord, yet even the dogs eat the crumbs that fall from their masters' table." Then Jesus answered her, "O woman, great is your faith! Be it done for you as you desire."[56]

This is an amazing passage as are so many of Jesus' teachings if we really take them in and allow them to do violence to our understanding. The woman is asking for a miracle concerning her

56. Matthew 15:21-28.

daughter, but she is not a Jew. How could she have faith if she is not of the right religious tradition? That is the thinking of religious people and it is even the thinking of Jesus' disciples who beg Jesus to send her away. Jesus uses this as a great teaching opportunity for his disciples. He takes their position and rebukes the woman for not being of the right religious tradition, but the woman then admonishes Jesus and tells him something of what she has learned about God. Jesus takes the admonishment and allows this woman of another religious tradition to refute what he had just said. What a valuable lesson about how we are to be open to having our understanding of God, and how God works, changed. Jesus responds to this woman's admonishment by telling us that here is a woman of *great faith*. She is open to seeing God at work in her life, and her understanding has come out of that experience and not out of her inherited religious tradition.

The faith that comes from trusting a religious tradition is the thing that Jesus is always preaching against. In Matthew's Gospel, Jesus tells his disciples, "Watch out and beware of the yeast of the Pharisees and Sadducees."[57] His disciples think that he mentions yeast because they had forgotten to bring bread with them (another pertinent example of how we are always missing what Jesus is saying). But, of course, he is speaking about the way our confidence in what we claim to know puffs us up as yeast makes bread to rise.

> "How could you fail to perceive that I was not speaking about bread? Beware of the yeast of the Pharisees and Sadducees! Then they understood that he had not told them to beware

57. Matthew 16:6.

> of the yeast of bread, but the teachings of the Pharisees and Sadducees."[58]

A confidence in their own understanding was what kept the religious people of Jesus' day from hearing what he was preaching, and it is still what keeps religious people from hearing what he is preaching. Real faith comes through the experience of God's mercy, which humbles us, while a belief in our own understanding puffs us up.

Faith as openness to seeing God at work in our lives is much closer to what Jesus means when he talks about faith than what we usually take faith to be. Like the religious leaders of Jesus' day, we often imagine that faith is an unwavering devotion to certain doctrines or theological traditions. This seems to be the real point of separation between people of faith. Some have faith in their religious traditions which teach them how God works, and others are open and able to see God feeding the dogs from the crumbs on the table. The differences between denominations is superficial in comparison to how much people are open or closed-minded concerning their understanding of God and their relationship to God. Of course, none of us are completely open or completely closed-minded. A major part of wisdom is to know what to be closed-minded about and what to be open-minded about. We need to be closed-minded about many things in order to simply function from day to day, but if we are closed-minded about everything, we have a very narrow experience of the Divine.

It can be puzzling to hear people who claim to have a personal relationship with Jesus but their theological understanding

58. Matthew 16:11-12.

of God has not changed in their lifetime. How is that possible? As we have said, personal relationships are dynamic, and our understanding of the other person changes with our intimate experience of them. This is why it is unrealistic to attempt to create unity within religious institutions by devotion to doctrinal beliefs, and the reason Jesus never establishes any. Openness to having our understanding changed by our God experiences is an essential characteristic of the faith journeys we see depicted in Scripture. Unfortunately, most Christian religions offer us theologies that are presented as certain, immutable, and the sacred means to salvation if we remain devoutly committed to that understanding. But the doctrines in which we put our faith have little to do with the teachings of Jesus. We don't see many Christian Churches with doctrines concerning, "Love your enemies"[59] or "If you forgive others their trespasses, your heavenly Father will also forgive you; but if you do not forgive others, neither will your Father forgive your trespasses."[60] If we did create doctrines out of his teachings we would find ourselves living in almost-constant states of repentance and equally constant states of experiencing God's mercy. Instead, we create doctrines that tell us how to be righteous before God so we can avoid repentance and the experience of mercy. By clinging to such doctrines we avoid the actual experience of God's mercy that would change our understanding of who God is.

This is the real difference between religious people. There are those who cling to their doctrines and traditions, and there are those who are open to having their experiences of the Divine change their understanding of God and themselves. This is what

59. Matthew 5:44.

60. Matthew 6:14-15.

separates people on spiritual matters. Jesus' disciples and the religious leaders of his day were both committed to the same religion, yet the disciples were open to having their understanding changed by Jesus while the religious leaders were not. If we would take seriously the things that Jesus says, we would be much more open-minded. If Jesus is open to being admonished and being told something about God by a Canaanite woman who isn't of his religion, what is the lesson we are to glean from this? Jesus uses this opportunity to show us that we should be open to ever more experiences of God's mercy, and how those experiences change our understanding. Unfortunately, most of our theologies provide us with boundaries: God is here and not there, he works this way and not that way. The more narrow and precise the theology the better, but the kind of faith of which Jesus speaks is much broader and more open than the theologies to which we are attracted.

This is certainly the case with the only other instance where Jesus says that someone has great faith. Again, it is someone outside of Jesus' own religious tradition: indeed, a Roman centurion.

> As he entered Capernaum, a centurion came forward to him, beseeching him and saying, "Lord, my servant is lying paralyzed at home, in terrible distress." And he said to him, "I will come and heal him." But the centurion answered him, "Lord, I am not worthy to have you come under my roof; but only say the word, and my servant will be healed. For I am a man under authority, with soldiers under me; and I say to one, `Go,' and he goes, and to another, `Come,' and he comes, and to my slave, `Do this,' and he does it." When Jesus heard him, he marveled, and said to those who followed him, "Truly, I

say to you, not even in Israel have I found such faith."[61]

As with the Canaanite woman, this instance of great faith has nothing to do with the kind of doctrinal religious beliefs that most consider religious faith today. Jesus' own faith was an awareness of a greater presence at work in his life, and he recognized a similar faith in the Canaanite woman and the Roman centurion. The Roman centurion tells Jesus of his own experience of having power because he is connected to the great power of Rome, and he recognizes that Jesus is under an even greater power. This kind of faith is not something we inherit or muster and then cling to for security. It is rather a faith that is produced in us through the experience of something greater than ourselves working in our interests. This is very different from the faith we have in our inherited theologies or religious traditions. That kind of faith is an understanding we grab onto and treat as sacred in order to believe that we are connected to truth itself, but it is merely one understanding among many possible understandings, and the truth of which Jesus speaks is much greater than we can think or imagine. The best we can do is to get glimpses of the Divine if we remain open and attentive to God at work in our lives.

Although Jesus calls the two instances above "great faith," the Gospel does reveal a faith that is even greater. It is a faith that humbles us because it is a faith that God provides through the very failure of what we think is our faith. There are at least two instances of this kind of faith in the Gospels. The first concerns Peter.

---

61. Matthew 8:5-13; Luke 7:1-10.

> And the Lord said, "Simon, Simon, behold, Satan hath desired to have you, that he may sift you as wheat: But I have prayed for thee, that thy faith fail not: and when thou art converted, strengthen thy brethren." And he said unto him, "Lord, I am ready to go with thee, both into prison, and to death." And he said, "I tell thee, Peter, the cock shall not crow this day, before that thou shalt thrice deny that thou knowest me."[62]

This is a strange passage since it appears that Peter's faith did fail that very night when Peter denied knowing Jesus three times. Jesus, however, says that he had prayed in order that Peter's faith would not fail. So, either Jesus is not very good at praying and Peter's faith did fail, or Jesus is good at praying and Peter's faith didn't fail even though he denied knowing Jesus three times. What Jesus knew was that Peter's denial was not a failure of his faith but part of a greater faith.

An additional thing that is extremely strange about the passage above is that Jesus says to Peter, "When thou art converted, strengthen thy brethren," but surely, Peter must have been converted already. He has spent three years with Jesus. He was on the Mount of Transfiguration[63] and saw Jesus transfigured and Moses and Elijah talking to him. He had walked on water at Jesus' command.[64] Peter had proclaimed that Jesus was "The Messiah, the Son of the living God;"[65] surely he must have been converted by such experiences. Jesus must be speaking of some deeper conversion—the kind that only God can provide when our attempts at faith fail.

---

62. Luke 22:31-34 KJV.
63. Matthew 17:1-13.
64. Matthew 14:28-32.
65. Matthew 16:16.

For Peter that deeper conversion begins on the night that Jesus was arrested. After professing that he was willing to die with Jesus, Peter denies ever having known him.[66] In that dark night what *we* might think was Peter's faith did fail, but Jesus seems to have known of a deeper faith that was not going to fail. In order to come to that deeper faith, Peter first had to come to see who he really was and who God really was, and that only comes about through a death and resurrection experience. Peter's faith—the faith that he mustered in order to believe and follow Jesus—had to die in order to receive the deeper faith that comes from God and not us. In order to see who we truly are, and who God is, the illusion of who we think we are must be destroyed. Peter thinks he knows who he is. He is a devout follower of Jesus for whom he is willing to die if necessary. But in that dark night, he discovers that despite his best intentions he was not able to sustain that faith. As Peter experiences the death of his own faith, and the death of who he thought he was, he is about to see who God truly is.

The revelation of who God truly is comes when Peter encounters the risen Christ. But it is not merely the fact that Peter has witnessed Jesus raised from the dead. What reveals the nature of God is the fact that the risen Christ never mentions Peter's denial, but instead gives Peter three chances to say, "I love you."[67] Most of us would have something to say to a friend who had failed so miserably in their faithfulness toward us. Jesus, however, never mentions Peter's denial. At that point, Peter must realize that nothing can separate him from Jesus' love, not even his own

66. John 18:17-27.

67. John 21:15-17.

unfaithfulness. Prior to that point, Peter might have known some things about Jesus, but it was not until his encounter with the risen Christ that he knew the true nature of the Divine and that nothing could separate him from God's love. This is the ultimate point of faith toward which we are all being drawn, but we only seem to reach it through that dark night of the soul when our own faith is shaken to its core. It is only when we experience God's love after our own faith has failed that we realize that God's love is not a response to our faith.

Of course, the ultimate manifestation of faith through death and resurrection is Jesus himself. In the Gospels, Jesus works miracles, heals the lame, and raises the dead. He does these things faithfully, but the end of his faith journey leads him into rejection, suffering, and what seems to be abandonment by God. This is the faith journey Jesus calls us to follow. It is a journey that eventually leads us to a place where we can only see one set of footprints and what appears to be God's absence. Jesus, from the cross, cries, "My God, my God, why have you forsaken me?"[68] Some argue that Jesus is merely quoting the twenty-second Psalm—which, no doubt he is—but he is also revealing the sense of abandonment that everyone who sets out on a genuine faith journey ultimately experiences.

There is a theology that claims that God did abandon Jesus because God cannot be in the presence of sin, and since Jesus had taken the sin of the world upon himself, God did in fact forsake Jesus. This is what we might believe before the deeper conversion. Our inherited, Christian understanding might have us believing

68. Matthew 27:46, and Mark 15:34.

that God loves the righteous and cannot tolerate sin. But Jesus' ministry is all about convincing us that none are righteous and all are sinners in need of God's forgiveness and mercy, which we receive because of who God is and not in exchange for something that we do or believe. The only way we come to that faith is when we are unable to muster any faith of our own and God seems a long way off.

It has been said that no one was more surprised on Easter Sunday morning than Jesus. To many that may seem blasphemous. Certainly, Jesus knew what was going to happen to him. He had prophesied what was going to happen, so it could not have been a surprise. But it was a surprise in the way that we are all surprised by what seems to be the absence of God in our hour of need. Jesus had never been distracted from an awareness of his Father's presence the way we so easily are by sin, but when Jesus took the sin of the world upon himself, he was distracted from an awareness of his Father's presence for the first time.

Jesus' response, however, is perfect. After experiencing what appears to be abandonment by God, Jesus says, "Father, into your hands I commend my spirit."[69] The next thing that happens is he wakes up alive in the tomb. This is the God experience that brings us to deep faith. It is the experience of feeling abandoned by God only to discover that God had been there all along. Jesus models this deep faith for us. The end of the faith journey is not death, but waking up alive in the tomb. This is the place we all come to, but some have come to that place before their physical death. If you have ever met a person who has been brought to that place

69. Luke 23:46.

of deep faith, they are different from the rest of us. They have been brought to a place where they see how little their faith is and how big God is. We all get to that place with physical death, but the most blessed of individuals experience it before their physical death, as did Peter. Unfortunately, many of us never let God take us that far, and faith remains something that we summon rather than something that God produces in us.

Today, many Christians' faith is, like the faith of the religious leaders in Jesus' day, a faith in their own understanding. What they trust is the way they have been taught to interpret sacred text and the doctrines that have been handed down to them by their religion. Such faith is epistemic and about what we know, but real faith is always beyond our knowing. Sadly, most don't want to experience this mystery of faith. We instead imagine that there is no mystery to it at all but simply a matter of us clinging to our deep convictions; however, the faith that comes from God is much deeper than our own understanding. It is not a belief that we cling to but an experience that is God-given when there appears to be nothing to which we can cling.

> Our faith begins at the point where atheists suppose that it must be at an end. Our faith begins with the bleakness and power which is the night of the cross, abandonment, temptation and doubt about everything that exists. Our faith must be born where it is abandoned by all tangible reality; it must be born of nothingness, it must taste this nothingness and be given it to taste in a way that no philosophy of nihilism can imagine.[70]

70. H. J. Iwand. Quoted in Jurgen Moltmann's, *The Crucified God.*

Or perhaps a still better understanding of it comes from Christian Wiman's claim that, "Revelation, like creation, arises not merely out of nothingness but *by means of it*."[71] Wiman goes on to say, "Faith is nothing more…than a motion of the soul toward God. It is not belief. Belief has objects—Christ was resurrected, God created the earth—faith does not. Even the motion of faith is mysterious and inexplicable."[72] Faith is simply that experience for which there is no explanation, and to insist upon an explanation is to truncate our human experience by our own will.

71. Christian Wiman. *My Bright Abyss*. New York: Farrar, Straus, and Giroux. 136.

72. Ibid. 139

CHAPTER SEVEN

Jesus on Sin

IN TRYING TO ARRIVE at some kind of understanding of the mind of Christ, and to take on the Jesus perspective for ourselves, we need to re-conceptualize our notions of religion, justice, wealth, family, and faith; but perhaps even most importantly, we need to come to grips with Jesus' concept of sin. With few exceptions, human beings have always understood sin as behavioral. Our human society rewards good behavior and punishes bad behavior. We don't send people to prison because of bad thoughts, but only bad behavior. Jesus, however, tells us that God knows and judges our hearts and it is therein that our sin lies. The reason God judges our hearts is because God desires what every lover desires from his or her beloved: that is, the beloved's attention. The Spanish philosopher, Jose Ortega y Gasset (1883-1955), claimed that love was essentially a matter of attention abnormally fixed.[73] His claim was that within the consciousness of the lover there is the constant presence of the beloved. This is certainly true of the love that exists between people who are romantically "in love." "For the lover his beloved . . . possesses a constant presence"[74] and

73. Jose Ortega y Gasset, *On Love: Aspects of a Single Theme,* trans. Toby Talbot (New York: Penguin Books, 1957), 64.

74. Ibid., 65.

occupies the lover's attention in a way that nothing else can.

In saying that "falling in love" is a phenomenon of attention, Ortega y Gasset is referring specifically to the romantic relationship between a man and a woman, but what he describes is also descriptive of other forms of love, and what we all desire in terms of being loved. The affection children desire from their parents largely involves attention. Even friendships, if they are to be meaningful, require that we are capable of fixing our attention upon our friend; if someone we consider a friend is unwilling to give us his or her attention, we may feel we may have been mistaken in considering that person a friend in the first place.

Unfortunately, however, as much as we desire the attention of spouses, parents, or friends, human beings are not very good at fixing their attention on any one individual for very long. The attention or focus of a normal human being is constantly changing from one thing to another. Because of this, we are a constant disappointment to our spouses, children, and friends. A wife's disappointment in her husband, as a lover, usually focuses on his lack of attention. "You're not here" is her complaint. And although he tries to assure her that he was listening and can even repeat what she said, her complaint is still true. He may have been listening, but he was not attentive. Small children seem instinctively to know the same thing about love and they evidence it by clamoring to their mothers, "Watch me!"

Of course, parents disappoint children, just as spouses disappoint one another, because human attention is fleeting even concerning the things we love most. Indeed, if a lover is one who fixes his attention on his beloved, then the vast majority of human beings make poor lovers. Fortunately, our desire to be loved by one who gives us extraordinary attention is not completely frustrated. God's omnipresent and omniscient nature makes him quite different from human beings. God is able to fix his attention on us in a way that other human beings are not. Unlike other human beings who constantly fail, God is perfectly attentive, but sadly we are seldom aware of it.

It is his nature that makes God the supreme lover and the only one who can truly satisfy our desire for attention. Of course, the attention he gives us is not mechanical, or merely the result of his omniscient and omnipresent nature. It is rather the result of his will. The Divine nature is one of awareness. That nature makes God aware of the whole of his creation, but he has chosen to fix his attention upon us as the centerpiece of that creation. Our potential to be made into divine lovers is what brings us into special focus.

This attention, which is an essential aspect of God's love toward us, is also an aspect of the kind of love that God wishes for us to have toward the Divine. Although existing in an imperfect degree in human beings, our love for God is largely a matter of attention just as his love toward us is largely a matter of attention. Indeed, we love God to the extent that God is in all our thoughts. Just as children measure the love of their parents by the amount and quality of the attention they give them, and wives measure the love of their husbands by their attention, we can measure our love toward God by attention as well. It is wise that we consider the measure of our attention toward God, for when we see how minuscule our attention is in comparison to his, we should be humbled and brought to a realistic perspective of who we are in relationship to God. Only from such a perspective do we see our true sin and what separates us from God.

There is a beautiful story in the tenth chapter of Luke's Gospel about Martha and Mary. Martha is the diligent sister who tries to do everything right in order to please Jesus as she welcomes him into her home. Her sister, Mary, doesn't help with all that Martha is trying to do to please Jesus, but rather simply sits at Jesus' feet and listens.

> But Martha was distracted by her many tasks; so she came to him and asked, "Lord, do you not care that my sister has left me to do all the work by myself? Tell her then to help me." But the Lord answered her, "Martha, Martha, you are worried and distracted by many things; there is need of only one thing. Mary has chosen the better part which will not be taken away from her."[75]

That one thing for which we have the greatest need is to simply dwell in his presence, but of course that is the most difficult thing, since we are constantly distracted from an awareness of that presence. That is our real sin—our only sin. It is what grieves the heart of God long before evil shows up in our behavior. We spend lives that are constantly distracted from an awareness of the Divine presence by all the petty affairs of this world, and fail to realize the fullness of life that comes from a constant awareness of God's presence. This is what grieves the heart of God.

We are all addicts. Some are addicted to drugs or alcohol, others to food or work. Some of our addictions are socially praiseworthy, while others are not, but the results are all the same: they all distract us from an awareness of the Divine presence. It is the Divine presence, and that presence alone, which is meant to be

75. Luke 10:38-42.

our addiction. Our other addictions and attachments are our real sin and what Jesus addresses in the Sermon on the Mount and throughout the rest of the Gospels.

If the first and great commandment is to love God, and if love is largely a matter of attention, then our great sin is our lack of attention toward God. Instead of fixing our attention upon God as Jesus did, our attention is abnormally fixed upon the things to which we become so easily attached and addicted. They are the distractions that constantly capture our attention and keep us from an awareness of God's presence. Some of those distractions are immoral by social standards, while some are praiseworthy, but they are all distractions that keep us from an awareness of the Divine presence. This is how Jesus seems to understand sin: that God's heart is grieved not by our behavior but by the fact that we are distracted by a great variety of things that divert our attention and keep us from an awareness of the Divine presence, and the fullness of life that comes with that awareness. This is our real sin: God is not in all of our thoughts. We are easily distracted by the things of this world, and that is why Jesus tells us that our sin is not murder but anger,[76] and not adultery but lust.[77] He goes on to warn us of other things like earthly treasure,[78] worry,[79] or judgment.[80] Jesus is revealing his unique concept of sin. He knows that what grieves the heart of God is that we worship the little gods of this world that own our attention in a way that only God should.

---

76. Matthew 5:21.
77. Matthew 5:27-28.
78. Matthew 6:19.
79. Matthew 6:25.
80. Matthew 7:1-2.

Anger, not murder, is the sin, because anger can easily become the god we look to as our source of energy and life. It is what motivates us. Athletes and other competitors often find strength and motivation in anger, while others live for vendetta. But Jesus tells us that it is God who is to be our source of strength.

Likewise, Jesus says, "You have heard that it was said, 'Do not commit adultery.' But I tell you that anyone who looks at a woman lustfully has already committed adultery with her in his heart."[81] Our contemporary culture sees nothing wrong with imagined infidelity, but Jesus tells us that our sin lies in the lust and not simply in the realization of the infidelity. That is because we turn our attention from an awareness of God's presence, not only when we engage in forbidden sex, but when we think about it. It is the lust or thought of sex that consumes our attention and turns our focus away from God. It is not the act of adultery that so displeases God that he turns away from us, but rather that we turn away from him when we fix our attention upon the things after which we lust.

The third thing that Jesus mentions in the Sermon on the Mount is that we are not to make oaths. Moses had given prohibitions against the breaking of oaths, but now Jesus tells us we should make no oaths at all.

> "You have heard that it was said to the people long ago, 'Do not break your oath, but keep the oaths you have made to the Lord.' But I tell you, Do not swear at all . . . . for you cannot make even one hair white or black."[82]

81. Matthew 5:27-28
82. Matthew 5:33-36.

First-century Christians saw pledging allegiance to anything other than God as a sin. The early Christian martyrs died not because they were Christians but because of their refusal to swear allegiance to pagan gods. You could be a Christian in the Roman Empire, but you had to pledge alliance to the Roman gods as well. It was *this* that the early Christians refused to do and they paid for it with their lives. The early Christians would never have pledged allegiance to the flag of the United States, because they took Jesus teachings seriously. Christians today are quite different. They want Jesus to be their Savior but not their Teacher and Master, and so they focus almost exclusively upon the last days of Jesus' life. They ignore the teachings and side with their culture, which purports that it is noble to keep our word and promises, even when those oaths cause us to end up on the side of evil. Of course, breaking our oaths is a problem as well. Thus, Jesus tells us to promise our commitment to nothing but God.[83]

The real problem with swearing oaths is that they, like anger and lust, are something we are quick to identify with and use as a source of energy and motivation. We boast to others and take pride in giving our word, as if there were a power in our words that enabled them to control circumstances. We would like to think that we are men or women of our word and, once given, our word is enough to motivate us to do what we have sworn. If we are honest with ourselves, however, we see what a lie that is, and how powerless our sworn oaths are. Jesus reminds us of that powerlessness and that we cannot make one hair white or black.[84] We, however, love the illusion of power within ourselves and therefore

83. Matthew 5:33-37.

84. Matthew 5:36.

swear oaths, as if we were able to control things with our will. God's desire is that we would draw our power from an awareness and identification with his presence.

Jesus next addresses our idea of retribution.

> "You have heard that it was said, 'Eye for eye, and tooth for tooth.' However, I tell you, Do not resist an evil person. If someone strikes you on the right cheek turn to him the other also."[85]

The Mosaic Law had allowed for retribution, which seems to provide human beings with some sense of satisfaction when injured by another, but it is a false sense of satisfaction. Real satisfaction or comfort comes from God alone. Of course, that requires the higher level of consciousness of which Jesus speaks. Additionally, our sense of justice that comes from retribution also gives us a false sense of righteousness. That we are just and not evil in doing to them what they did to us, but of course, if it were evil for them to do it, it is evil for us as well.

What Jesus says next probably goes farther beyond what Moses had given in the law than anything else Jesus ever said. The people of the Old Testament were not ready to receive this commandment, just as most of us are still not ready to receive it today.

> "You have heard that it was said, 'Love your neighbor and hate your enemies.' But I tell you: Love your enemies and pray for those who persecute you that you may be sons of your Father in heaven."[86]

---

85. Matthew 5:38-39.
86. Matthew 5:43-45.

This is not merely a difficult commandment; it is an *a priori* impossibility. Enemies are by definition people we do not love. If we love our enemies, the idea of an "enemy" loses its meaning. Perhaps Jesus could ask us not to take revenge upon our enemies, or maybe even not to hate them, but to love them seems beyond the realm of human possibility. That, however, is just the point. What Jesus presents in the Sermon on the Mount, and for the most part throughout the rest of the Gospel as well, is a divine standard or level of consciousness that is so far beyond us that it should keep us in a perpetual state of repentance and, consequently, the ongoing experience of God's mercy.

Following the command to love our enemies, Jesus then begins to instruct us concerning religious activities. When we give to the needy, we should do it in such a way that that doesn't gain us recognition from others. Thus, it is not enough that we give, but we must give with the right attitude, and that right attitude is that we give without a desire for recognition. This may seem strange since previously Jesus said, "Let your light shine before men, that they might see your good deeds and praise your father in heaven."[87] Obviously, if we give with the intent of others seeing our good deeds, it is not a good deed; indeed, it is our pretense to righteousness which Jesus constantly condemns. Whenever Jesus praises someone, as he did with the Roman Centurion and the Canaanite woman, it is never for something that human beings recognize as praiseworthy. We do not recognize anything exceptionally praiseworthy about the insights of the Centurion or Canaanite woman, but that is because they do not conform to our human prejudices

87. Matthew 5:16.

concerning worth or value. This is why we dismiss most of Jesus teachings: they represent a divine standard or level of consciousness that is simply too alien for us. There is a human motivation for charity which is prestige and reputation, but the divine motivation is mercy. Jesus is constantly calling us to a divine level of consciousness of which we are oblivious because we cling so tightly to the sacred prejudices that make up our all-too-human consciousness. Indeed, our human standards make us feel good about ourselves, but the divine standards Jesus sets forth make us aware of our infinite need for repentance and the experience of God's mercy.

There is a similar situation with the religious practices of prayer and fasting. As with almsgiving, Jesus tells us we are to do it in a way that no one but God knows. It is not enough that we pray and fast, but we must do it without reputation or esteem being our motivation. Our value and worth comes from God alone and to think it could come from any other source is an illusion. Jesus is trying to show us that what grieves the heart of God is not doing what human beings consider evil, but that we try to find life and happiness through being esteemed by human beings rather than God. We are constantly being distracted from an awareness of the Divine presence and the fullness of life that comes from that awareness. This is the root of all sin: that we try to find life and identity apart from God.

In a similar manner, Jesus instructs us concerning earthly treasure. Like fame and recognition among human beings, we look to earthly treasure rather than God as a source of life and identity. But Jesus tells us that such treasures are a fleeting source of worth, and we will soon be disappointed if we attempt to draw life from them. He says,

> "Do not store up for yourselves treasures on earth, where moth and rust destroy, and where thieves break in and steal. But store up for yourselves treasures in heaven, where neither moth nor rust consumes and where thieves do not break in and steal. For where your treasure is there your heart will be also."[88]

The next thing Jesus addresses in the Sermon on the Mount is worry. Certainly, being frightened is not a sin, but as we allow what scares us to remain in our lives and become worry, we certainly do sin, since our worry easily becomes the thing that monopolizes our attention and distances us from an awareness of God's presence. Anxiety is the opposite of the kind of faith to which Jesus calls us. When we are anxious about many things, it is very difficult to be aware of God's presence. With worry at the center of our being, God is not in all of our thoughts, and it is not God, but worry, that energizes and defines us. For many people, worry is their source of identity and it occupies the place that should be reserved for God alone.

Finally, Jesus says, "Do not judge."[89] That, however, is what we most want to do. What is behind so much of our theology is a desire to have a standard by which we can judge the saved from the unsaved, the godly from the ungodly, and the moral from the immoral. We think we can judge what is good and what is evil, but the truth is that we form our judgments based on insufficient understanding, which is the limited perspective we draw from our inherited human prejudices and the level of consciousness that they create. God's perspective is very different.

---

88. Matthew 6:19-21.
89. Matthew 7:1.

The serpent may have told Adam and Eve that if they ate the forbidden fruit they would know as God knows,[90] but that was a lie. Not everything in the Bible is true. Our theory about what it means for the Bible to be God-breathed should not exclude the possibility of God revealing lies in the Bible. What the serpent told Adam and Eve was certainly a lie. We lack God's eternal perspective, and therefore cannot tell the wheat from the weeds. Sadly, what religion so often offers is an understanding that makes us feel that we are capable of making judgments concerning righteousness. By contrast, any serious reading of the Sermon on the Mount should convince us that Jesus' understanding of sin and righteousness is very different from our own, and therefore any judgments we make based on our understanding are going to be very different from Jesus' judgments. Jesus' warning against judgments ends his litany on sin and righteousness. He then concludes the Sermon on the Mount by saying,

> "Ask and it will be given to you; seek and you will find; knock and the door will be opened to you. For everyone who asks receives; he who seeks finds; and to him who knocks, the door will be opened."[91]

In light of the impossible standard that Jesus has set forth in the Sermon on the Mount, it seems obvious that what we need to ask and seek is that God would extend mercy toward us for having failed to live by the standard that Jesus sets forth. What we need to ask is that God would give us a spirit of repentance in order that we can turn away from the false gods of this world

90. Genesis 3:4-5.
91. Matthew 7:7-8.

and experience God's presence through the mercy that he constantly extends. We will always be distracted from an awareness of God's presence by the false gods and false sources of life that we constantly encounter in this world. What we need is a grace that will allow us to never tire of repentance, so we can continually turn away from those things that fuel the false self, and therein turn back toward God, who is the ultimate source of our life and identity. God is willing to provide all the forgiveness and mercy we need; all we need to do is be willing to live in a state of almost-constant repentance. If we simply have to ask, then what we need to ask is that we will be filled with a spirit of repentance, and a constant turning away from all those things that so easily entrap us and keep us from drawing our strength and energy—our life and meaning—from God alone.

The good news is that God is not calling us to obey a moral law of endless requirements. He is calling us to a relationship, and that relationship is not sustained by our goodness but by God's mercy alone. Sadly, many people live lives unaware of the Divine presence because they are constantly distracted by all the things Jesus speaks of in the Sermon on the Mount. They seek happiness in their earthly treasure and in the reputations they have taken so long to acquire. They like the life that comes from their lust, anger, and even their worry. These things define them and they cannot imagine an identity apart from them. It is all that they are, and they feel that without these things, they would be nothing. It is in our nothingness, however, that we find the God who is our real source of identity, meaning, purpose, and life.

As has already been said, our concept of sin is very different from Jesus' concept. We imagine sin to be behavioral, but

Jesus is obviously talking about something very different here in the Sermon on the Mount. If he was pointing to anger as sinful behavior, rather than the thing upon which we focus and draw life from rather than God, then Jesus failed to live by his own teachings when he chased the money changers from the Temple with what appears to be angry behavior.[92] Likewise, on the Mount of Olives before his arrest, Luke's Gospel tells us that he was in anguish and sweat blood.[93] Such behavior certainly seems to be a manifestation of worry. And in John's Gospel the entire seventeenth chapter has Jesus praying publically in front of his disciples, which he warns against in the Sermon on the Mount.[94] So either Jesus fails to live by his own teachings, or the Sermon on the Mount is a matter of Jesus telling us that our sin in not in our behavior. Rather he is identifying those things that most commonly capture our attention and keep us from an awareness of the Divine presence. That is the common denominator among things such as anger, lust, enemies, good works, earthly treasure, and worry. These are the things from which we attempt to draw life rather than God. They are the distractions that keep us from an awareness of God's presence and the fullness of life that comes with that awareness.

A central theme that runs throughout the Gospels is Jesus' awareness of the Divine presence that he refers to as his heavenly father. A great part of his ministry is focused upon teaching us to practice an awareness of that presence. This is what the great saints have understood: that we are still in the Garden, and, like Adam,

92. Matthew 21:12-13.

93. Luke 22:44.

94. Matthew 6:5-6.

God still walks with us, but none of us lives in an awareness of that Divine presence the way Jesus did. We do occasionally achieve such states of awareness in prayer, but it is fleeting. The fact that it is fleeting reveals the depth of our sin as nothing else can. Only as we attempt to focus our attention upon God's presence in the way that being in love entails, do we discover what inept lovers we are. We are distracted by just about anything, and when we try to really pray and focus our attention upon God, we find that thirty seconds is a long time to go without being distracted by those ideas that constantly invade our consciousness. Imagine a situation in which you profess to love someone, but you are only able to give your attention to that person for thirty seconds at a time. Imagine how frustrated that person would be with your attempt at loving him or her. Fortunately, unlike a human lover who would respond by finding someone else, God's response is always mercy.

The experience of prayer, or the practice of God's presence, should convince us that we are incapable of the great commandment to love God with our whole heart, soul, mind, and strength. The experience of that failure, however, is the very thing that leads us to the experience of mercy, and it is the experience of mercy that is at the heart of the transformation that makes us into his likeness. Those who spend much time in deep prayer recognize their need for mercy more than the rest of us, since they recognize how easily their attention is diverted and how they constantly fail to give God the attention that a love relationship requires.

When we compare ourselves to other human beings we can all too easily imagine ourselves as righteous; when we compare ourselves to Jesus and the way he was never distracted from an awareness of the Divine presence by all the things that distract us, we see our great need for mercy. The good news, however, is that our lack of attention and God's judgment of it is not something that condemns us, but something meant to bring us to repentance and the experience of God's mercy. Only by being the constant recipients of mercy do we become merciful as he is merciful.

We do not, however, need to increase sinful behavior in order to increase our experience of mercy. We simply need to see the depth of our sin by taking seriously the teachings of Jesus. This is our real sin: that our attention is fixed upon the distractions of this world rather than God.

> "The eye is the lamp of the body. So, if your eye is healthy, your whole body will be full of light, but if your eye is unhealthy, your whole body will be full of darkness."[95]

We equate darkness with our cultural concept of evil, but Jesus is talking about something much more subtle. The darkness of which he speaks is simply a matter of those things that distract us from an awareness of God's presence. If we set our eyes constantly upon God and remain focused upon an awareness of his presence, we are full of light, but if our eye is focused upon all the distractions of this world, then we are full of darkness.

The point of the Sermon on the Mount, and so many of Jesus' other teachings, is that our claims to righteousness are always based upon our cultural concepts of sin and evil. If we were ever to consider the divine standard Jesus sets forth, we would see that none are righteous and all are in need of mercy. This is the great leveler that puts us all in the same place before God. We are all

95. Matthew 6:22-23.

in need of mercy, and therefore we cannot look down upon our sisters and brothers who do not meet our standards because we know that none of us meet God's standard. When we see what sin is really all about, we realize that as much as we clean up our behavior, our hearts are prone to wander from the God we love, and we never get beyond our need for mercy. Consider the parable Jesus tells of the Banquet.

> "A certain man was preparing a great banquet and invited many guests. At the time of the banquet he sent his servant to tell those who had been invited, 'Come, for everything is now ready.' But they all alike began to make excuses. The first said, 'I have just bought a field, and I must go and see it. Please excuse me.' Another said, 'I have just bought five yoke of oxen, and I'm on my way to try them out. Please excuse me.' Still another said, 'I just got married, so I can't come.' "[96]

Notice that those who choose not to be at the banquet do so as a result of their choice to be somewhere else. Furthermore, it is interesting that the "somewhere else" we choose to be is not the crack house or bordello, but they are busy doing what we consider good things like getting married or doing business. Certainly these are not the kinds of things God would condemn us for. Certainly not! God does not condemn us or exclude us from his great banquet at all, but rather we excuse ourselves from his presence. But although we choose things other than God to love and focus our attention upon rather than being aware of his presence, God's love for us endures through the mercy he constantly extends.

---

96. Luke 14:16-20 NIV.

If we truly followed Jesus' example, we would all be dwelling in a constant awareness of the Divine presence. Of course, none of us do; therefore none of us can claim righteousness. Even those with the most perfect behavior among us must come through God's mercy. Our hearts are prone to wander, and God is not in all their thoughts. Our sin that grieves the heart of God is that we choose to be caught up in all the petty distractions of this world rather than the fullness of life that comes with a constant awareness of his presence.

We almost always begin a relationship with God by seeking a means to become righteous in God's sight. What we eventually discover, however, is that God loves us in the midst of our sin. Furthermore, he desires that we become creatures who can love others in the midst of their sin. The best way to accomplish that is by seeing how deep our sin goes, and experiencing God's love in the midst of that sin. We can fool ourselves into thinking we are righteous if we hold onto our cultural notion of sin, but if we embrace Jesus' concept of sin, we see that there is no escape from it, and we must learn to live in a constant state of repentance and the experience of his mercy. We must come to see that our real sin is the flaw or crack that lets in the light of God's mercy, which, if experienced enough, eventually starts to make us into his merciful likeness.

The problem with so many of the churches that bear Jesus' name is that they have concocted theologies that show us how to become righteous rather than merciful. But if we ever allowed Jesus' teachings to do violence to our cultural understanding, and bring us to that higher level of divine consciousness that is the mind of Christ, we would see that the Gospel is not about righteousness, but rather about mercy. If we would ever recognize this, the virus of the Gospel would infect the world. However, that has not been our history; we are still very far from taking on the mind of Christ.

CHAPTER EIGHT

Jesus on Repentance

JESUS BEGINS HIS public ministry by preaching repentance. "From that time Jesus began to proclaim, 'Repent, for the kingdom of heaven has come near.'"[97] The Greek word here that is translated as repent is *μετανοεῖτε*. The prefix *μετα* can be translated as *after* or *beyond*, and νοεῖτεο refers to *mind*. Perhaps the best translation is to rethink or think again. Of course, Christian churches have largely understood repentance as a turning away from sinful behavior and toward righteousness, but Jesus' concept of repentance is very different. Our concept of repentance is certainly tied to our idea of sin, and if our idea of sin is essentially immoral behavior then it is natural that we would suppose repentance to be a matter of correcting immoral behavior. Of course, as we saw in the last chapter, Jesus' concept of sin is very different from what many Christians imagine. Jesus has a radical concept of sin and an equally radical concept of repentance. Like so many of Jesus' concepts, his concept of repentance goes against sacred prejudices that people in his day, as well as our own, believed were essential to hold society together.

In the world of Jesus' day, social order was maintained through what anthropologists refer to as an honor/shame-based

97. Matthew 4:17.

culture. In such a world, social order is maintained by avoiding behavior that would be shameful and cause one to be ostracized, and instead demonstrating behavior that would bring one honor in the community. There is an element of that in our own society today, although a legal system is also used to enforce the social order. As it is today, the social order in Jesus' day was sexist, with different standards for men and women as to what behavior is honorable and what is shameful. Remember the woman caught in adultery who is brought before Jesus?[98] They do not bring the man as well, since adultery in that society was more shameful for a woman. A promiscuous man is often seen in a different light than a promiscuous woman.

In such a society, shameful behavior put you at the bottom of society and honorable behavior put you at the top. Jesus is constantly defying such a social order and doing things that are associated with shame rather than honor. He doesn't honor the Sabbath the way a religious Jew of his day was expected to, he doesn't observe the dietary laws, and he associates with sinners and other shameful types that honorable people were expected to avoid, since association with them meant that you were shameful as well. Jesus is obviously defying this honor/shame-based social order because he knows it for the lie it is.

Unfortunately, most Christian denominations tell their people to avoid shameful behavior and seek to do what is honorable, but Jesus tells us we should repent for honorable behavior as well. The reason for this is that Jesus knows that our righteousness is a pretense. Jesus knows that we are all sinners, and the blessed ones

98. John 8:1-11.

are those who recognize their sin and practice repentance in order to experience God's mercy. Those who consider themselves honorable miss that experience and its transformative power. That is why Jesus is constantly trying to expose hypocrisy and bring us all to the place of seeing our need for repentance and the experience of God's mercy.

> The Pharisees, who were lovers of money, heard all this, and they ridiculed him. So he said to them, "You are those who justify yourselves in the sight of others, but God knows your hearts; for what is prized by human beings is an abomination in the sight of God."[99]

Why is it that what is honorable to human beings is an abomination to God? It is because God knows our hearts and is not fooled by our behavior. He knows that our pretense to righteousness is just that—a pretense for which we need to repent. Indeed, if we really wish to know ourselves apart from the image we portray to others, we would need to take Jesus' words seriously and begin to repent and change our minds about almost everything. Of course, we don't allow Jesus' words to make such drastic changes in our lives, and we merely tailor a tribal Jesus who fits into the honor/shame culture we inherit. We can't hear Jesus speaking out against an honor/shame-based social order because that is a large part of our inherited understanding.

Indeed, to really see what the Jesus message is all about, we have to alter our thinking in order to recognize that what is valued by human beings is an abomination to God. Likewise, we need to see that some things that we negatively value, God sees as

99. Luke 16:15.

virtuous. Repentance is certainly one such thing. Since our honor/shame-based culture tells us that righteousness is good and sin is bad, we see repentance as evidence of our sin, and therefore something to be avoided. The ideal is not to sin at all, and thereby not to be in need of repentance. But God's ultimate purpose is to make us into his merciful likeness. In order for that to happen, we must experience much mercy, and to do so, we must see almost everything as an opportunity for repentance.

An example of this is the twenty-fifth chapter of Matthew's Gospel. In that chapter, Jesus gives us three parables: the parable of the virgins with the lamps, the parable of the talents, and the parable of the sheep and the goats. The standard reading of the first parable is that the wise virgins who took enough oil for their lamps were good and rewarded, while the unprepared virgins who did not have enough oil were foolish and therefore suffered exclusion from the wedding feast.

What should be of concern about this first parable is the fact that the ten wise virgins do not share their oil with their sisters who are in need. That does not seem like the Christian thing to do. They do not act charitably, but think only of themselves. Furthermore, the parable begins by Jesus continuing his talk about the end of the age. He says at the beginning of chapter twenty-five, "At that time the kingdom of heaven will be like ten virgins who took their lamps and went out to meet the bridegroom." He describes what the kingdom of heaven and those who are his followers at that time will be like, but is their behavior prescriptive, or does it merely represent the self-interest of God's people at the end of the age? Should they have only thought of their own interest and not the interest of the others, who, although foolish, also wished to greet the bridegroom? This sounds very reminiscent of those who want Jesus all for themselves. They do not share the source of the light within them with others, even though others may end up outside the great banquet because the virgins with the oil refused to share. Of course, their excuse is that if they did share their own lights might go out—as if the source of light within us is measured, and we have to be stingy with our spiritual light. The Gospel tells us that, as we give our light away, God provides more light within us. True, the idea of getting more by giving away does run contrary to the way we think—as does almost everything in the Gospels.

It is very easy to miss the point of this parable because we are always looking to see who is right and who is wrong. Jesus' point, however, seems to be that both sides in the parable are wrong. It was foolish for the virgins not to have oil, but it was also selfish for the wise virgins not to share. One sins because of their foolishness, the other because of their selfishness. We are all sinners in need of repentance. That is the central message of the Gospel, but we often miss that because of our left-brain, either/or approach to situations: we look to see who is right and who is wrong. That is how we generally approach everything, including the Gospel. We believe Jesus must be showing us how to do things in a right way, and therefore is depicting people doing things right and people doing things wrong. Within a society where it is good to be industrious, it is easy to see that the lazy virgins are wrong (which they are), but we then quickly assume that if they are wrong, the other virgins must be right. One is the saint and the other the sinner. Jesus, however, tells us we are all sinners in need of repentance.

Of course, Jesus also tells us that we are all saints,[100] or better than saints, as we are daughters and sons of God and nothing can separate us from his love. That contradiction is hard on our left-brain, either/or logic. We want to find favor with God by doing the right thing, but according to Jesus the right thing is to see our sin, respond through repentance, and come to the experience of God's mercy.

That is not usually appealing to human beings. We like the idea of merit. We are always trying to distinguish ourselves in order to be convinced of our superiority. We are always judging the good from the bad and finding ourselves good and other people bad, but Jesus tells us that we are all both wheat and tares.[101] The tares in our lives have a purpose, and are the very things that bring us to repentance and the experience of God's mercy. Without an awareness of the tares, we become like the religious leaders of Jesus' day who thought they were pure wheat and without need of repentance, forgiveness, and mercy.

We, too, think we are wise enough to know the tares from the wheat, but of course, we are not. We imagine that God wants us to be good. Our parents always told us to be good, so we imagine

100. "In my life I find that I am, in the classic phrase, *simul justus et peccator,* both justified and a sinner. That is to say, I find that my life has been totally transformed by being one with Christ. And yet I find that I still fall into the same old patterns of sin. This is not even a matter of percentages—x percent better, y percent still sinful. Rather, I really am totally transformed, even on those days when I am just as much a sinner as if I were not redeemed at all. It is indeed puzzling how that should be possible, and yet I know it to be true." William Placher, "Christ Takes Our Place: Rethinking Atonement." *Interpretations*. Vol.53. No.1 (1999): 11.

101. Matthew 13:24-30.

that God must want the same thing. At times, however, we find ourselves in situations where there is no good choice. Someone in ministry was once asked how it could be possible to handle a situation that did not involve a choice between good and evil, but only a choice between evil and evil. That is, that there was no good choice but simply two bad choices. His response was that God would never let that happen and would always provide a good option for us to take. Of course, that's not true, and often we find ourselves in circumstances where it is a choice between two evils. We usually choose the lesser evil and call it good since we see good and evil as corollaries, and if one choice is evil the other must be good. Certainly, we should always choose the lesser of the two evils, but instead of calling it good, we should see it for the evil it is and use that as an opportunity for repentance and a further experience of God's forgiveness and mercy. For example, people often respond to those who advocate for nonviolence with a question such as this: "What if someone was attacking your wife or kids? You wouldn't use violence to stop them?" Of course, but don't call it good simply because it is the lesser of two evils. There are times when violence may be necessary, but we should then use it as an opportunity for repentance and the experience of forgiveness rather than calling it good.

There is a similar situation with the second parable of that chapter. There Jesus tells a story about a man going on a journey and entrusting his slaves with his property. To one he gave five talents,[102] to another two, and to another one, according to their ability. When the master returns he rewards the first slave

102. A talent was the largest unit of money in Jesus' day. Scholars estimate it to have been the equivalent of between $1,000 and $30,000.

who invested the talents and made five more talents. Likewise, he rewards the second slave who invested his two talents and made two more talents. The third slave, however, did not invest his talent for fear. For he says,

> " 'Master, I knew that you were a harsh man, reaping where you did not sow, and gathering where you did not scatter seed; so I was afraid, and I went and hid your talent in the ground. Here is yours.' But his master replied, 'You wicked and lazy slave! You knew, did you, that I reap where I did not sow, and gather where I did not scatter seed? Then you ought to have invested my money with the bankers, and on my return I would have received what was my own with interest. So take the talent from him, and give it to the one with ten talents. For to all those who have, more will be given, and they will have an abundance; but from those who have nothing, even what they have will be taken away. As for this worthless slave, throw him into the outer darkness, where there will be weeping and gnashing of teeth.' "[103]

A typical reading of this imagines that the master in the parable represents God, and he rewards and punishes based upon merit. It is easy to interpret the Scripture in that way, since we live in a capitalistic society which sees merit and profit as basic values, but the Gospel runs contrary to a merit system. According to the Gospel, the last will be first and the first last,[104] and the one who labors only the last hour gets the same wage as those who labored all day.[105]

---

103. Matthew 25:24-30.
104. Matthew 19:30 & 20:16.
105. Matthew 20:1-16.

There are numerous other problems with reading this Scripture from the perspective of reward and punishment. For one thing, God is not a harsh master who reaps where he does not sow. Human beings may be harsh and take from the poor who have little and give it to those who already have much. Indeed, the master in the story of the talents seems very typical of the masters of today's world, who also take from those who have little and give to those who have much. Interestingly, in Matthew's Gospel, both chapters twenty-four and twenty-five are dealing with Jesus' description of the end times.

Yet another problem with such a reading is that this story of the talents in Matthew's Gospel is very much like the story in the nineteenth chapter of Luke's Gospel. There Jesus says, "A nobleman went to get royal power for himself and then return."[106] Liberation theologians read that parable as being about Herod's son who in fact in Jesus' day went off to a distant country (Rome) to be made ruler in Palestine. Jesus even says, "But the citizens of his country hated him and sent a delegation after him saying, 'we do not want this man to rule over us.'"[107] In this parable, before the nobleman left, he took ten of his servants and gave them ten pounds, instructing them to put the money to work. When he returned, he rewarded the servant who made ten more pounds by putting him in charge of ten cities. Likewise, the servant who made five more pounds, he put in charge of five cities. One of the servants, however, buried his pound as in the parable from Matthew's Gospel. As with Matthew's Gospel, the servant who buried the money says,

---

106. Luke 19:12.
107. Luke 19:14.

> I was afraid of you, because you are a harsh man; you take what you did not deposit, and reap what you did not sow.[108]

The ruler punishes the servant who did not produce a profit, and he takes the pound from him and gives it to the man with ten pounds. The bystanders respond by saying, but he already has ten pounds. To which the ruler responds,

> I tell you to all those who have, more will be given; but from those who have nothing, even what they have will be taken away. But as for these enemies of mine who did not want me to be king over them—bring them here and slaughter them in my presence.[109]

That might fit very nicely with what we would like to think is the nature of God, since it is very compatible with our contemporary culture. However, it is a very different god from the one whom Jesus is describing throughout the Gospels. As we have said, God is not harsh and does not reap where he does not sow. This is clearly a picture of the world in which Jesus lived, where those who had much were given more, and those who had little had even that taken from them. That was Jesus' world, and it is still our world today.

Of course, the other interpretation is not necessarily *bad*; in fact, it is a starting point for those who live in a capitalist, competitive society. It is their initial interpretation of who God is, and we all need some initial understanding, misguided as it might be. It is a place to start our journey in pursuit of the divine. If we had

108. Luke 19:21.

109. Luke 19:26-27.

to have a *right* understanding of God from the very beginning, none of us would ever have a relationship with God. All personal relationships begin in misunderstanding. A personal knowledge of someone with whom we are in relationship grows over time, and if it doesn't grow over time that indicates that it is not a personal relationship. How strange that there are people who claim to have a personal relationship with Jesus when their theology hasn't changed in forty years. Personal relationships are journeys which require that we continually move ever deeper into an understanding of that other person. In looking back on a personal relationship, many of our previous understandings may seem flawed as a result of the deeper insights we have now attained, but those earlier perspectives were necessary, and part of getting to know the person. Thus, we can appreciate even what we might later consider "wrong" perspectives if we consider them essential parts of the journey. Even the beginnings of the journey are a holy place.

We somehow think that the point is to have the perfect understanding or the right theology, but it is much more important that we become like him in terms of mercy. We began this text with this third parable in this twenty-fifth chapter of Matthew's Gospel because of its centrality to mercy, but this parable is also central to pointing out two other essential things as well. Recall what Jesus says,

> "When the Son of Man comes in His glory, and all the holy angels with Him, then He will sit on the throne of His glory. All the nations will be gathered before Him, and He will separate them one from another, as a shepherd divides *his* sheep from the goats. And He will set the sheep on His right hand, but the goats on the left. Then the King will say to those on

> His right hand, 'Come, you blessed of My Father, inherit the kingdom prepared for you from the foundation of the world: for I was hungry and you gave Me food; I was thirsty and you gave Me drink; I was a stranger and you took Me in; I was naked and you clothed Me; I was sick and you visited Me; I was in prison and you came to Me.' Then the righteous will answer Him, saying, 'Lord, when did we see You hungry and feed You, or thirsty and give You drink? When did we see You a stranger and take You in, or naked and clothe You? Or when did we see You sick, or in prison, and come to You?' And the King will answer and say to them, 'Assuredly, I say to you, inasmuch as you did it to one of the least of these My brethren, you did it to Me.' Then He will also say to those on the left hand, 'Depart from Me, you cursed, into the everlasting fire prepared for the devil and his angels: for I was hungry and you gave Me no food; I was thirsty and you gave Me no drink; I was a stranger and you did not take Me in, naked and you did not clothe Me, sick and in prison and you did not visit Me.' Then they also will answer Him, saying, 'Lord, when did we see You hungry or thirsty or a stranger or naked or sick or in prison, and did not minister to You?' Then He will answer them, saying, 'Assuredly, I say to you, inasmuch as you did not do it to one of the least of these, you did not do it to Me.'"[110]

Notice that both the sheep and goats were wrong in terms of their understanding. Neither one knew what the Lord wanted from them. They both needed to repent or change their minds regarding their understanding. Additionally, the other thing that is apparent

110. Matthew 25:31-45 NKJV.

from this parable is how wrong we are to think that God wants us to work out of a system of reward and punishment. When the sheep extended mercy to those in need, they did not do it for any thought of a reward since those who were hungry, thirsty, naked, sick, and in prison had no means to reward them. They did what they did because they had become merciful, and not because they thought their behavior was going to be rewarded. Likewise, the goats did operate out of a reward/punishment system since they would have never neglected doing such things for the King who had the power to reward or punish, while those they saw in need had no such power. One of the main points to be drawn from this parable is that those who operate under a reward/punishment system will be very disappointed for having lived their lives by doing what they think will bring reward and avoid punishment rather than becoming merciful as God is merciful.

The other thing that is to be gleaned from this parable is how antireligious it is. The sheep had no idea they were doing something that was pleasing to God, and likewise the goats had no idea they were neglecting something that was important to God. Remember, a common religious belief that persists to our present day is that people who find themselves hungry, naked, sick, or in prison are in those situations because of sin. This is a common religious prejudice against which Jesus is always preaching.

With this parable, as with the other two, both sides should see their need for repentance or changing their minds. Neither the goats nor the sheep saw the divine image in those who were hungry, thirsty, naked, sick, or in prison. Both groups should have seen that as an opportunity for repentance. The goats, however, have another reason to repent in that they are inside a reward and punishment system in which there is no way to win. If we think that righteousness is anything more than becoming merciful, we really don't understand Jesus' concept of sin and righteousness. The intention behind nearly all of Jesus' teachings is to bring us to repentance; that is, to change our focus and fix our attention on God's presence and see that presence in everything.

We miss this point because we read Jesus' teachings with an eye to see how *right* we are and how *wrong* others are. We want to be right before God, but the only way to be right before God is to realize our need for repentance, and to allow that to bring us into an ever-deeper awareness of his forgiveness and mercy. This is not very appealing to religious types. Listen to the way people who consider themselves righteous speak about sinners. Remember the girl at the Christian college who couldn't understand the other girls in her dorm reaching out to the girl who had gotten pregnant. They were rewarding the pregnant girl's sinful behavior and she couldn't understand that. People who seek to be righteous rather than merciful will always try to establish their righteousness by comparing themselves to those who they consider sinners rather than comparing themselves to Jesus. When we compare ourselves to Jesus we have to give up our idea of righteousness and begin to seek mercy. God's kingdom is founded upon mercy, and our world would be much more divine if our religions were focused on repentance and the experience of mercy rather than the pursuit of righteousness.

Jesus is turning the world upside down. We naturally see our love of family, justice, wealth, and religion as good things, while Jesus tells us that such things are what should bring us to repentance. We think we can avoid sin and therefore should have no need of repentance, but that is because we understand neither Jesus' concepts of sin or repentance. Throughout Jesus' teachings, he continually reinforces the fact that we are all sinners in need of repentance and the experience of God's mercy. Christians who talk about homosexuality or abortion in a disparaging way are no doubt doing so to make themselves feel righteous. And if it does, that's a problem, because it means that they have almost no idea of Jesus' teachings. Jesus very specifically addresses the fallacy of assuming that some sinners are greater sinners than others, and of comparing ourselves to the *terrible sinners* so that we can feel righteous.

> At that very time there were some present who told him about the Galileans whose blood Pilate had mingled with their sacrifices. He asked them, "Do you think that because these Galileans suffered in this way they were worse sinners than all other Galileans? No, I tell you; but unless you repent, you will all perish as they did. Or those eighteen who were killed when the tower of Siloam fell on them—do you think that they were worse offenders than all others living in Jerusalem? No, I tell you, but unless you repent you will all perish just as they did."[111]

In the middle of the AIDS epidemic, we heard Christians proclaiming that it was God's response to homosexuality, as if that sin were greater than their own. Jesus is very clear about everyone's need of repentance and not just those that we think commit the most grievous sins by our particular cultural standards. Jesus says that he has "come to call not the righteous but sinners to

111. Luke 13:1-5.

repentance."[112] Sadly, many people are only able to see the sins of others and miss out on the divine experience of mercy.

Jesus never condemns, nor does he even speak harshly toward anyone for their sins. The only ones he does condemn and speak harshly toward are those who think that they have no sin and are not in need of repentance. Churches may preach repentance, but only to the outsider who has yet to accept that particular church's formula for righteousness. They preach repentance to those who have not yet accepted their theology but, for those who have, they are told that they have been given a path to righteousness. Some even create doctrines that tell followers that God forgives them for all of their sins (past, present, and future) at the moment of their conversion, and that they no longer have need for ongoing and constant repentance. Their theologies assure them that they can find righteousness in their beliefs and therefore avoid any further need of repentance or changing their minds (*metanoia*). It is their theology, rather than the teachings of Jesus, that becomes sacred. For many churches, to be saved by faith has come to mean that their members have the *right* beliefs or theology rather than having the kind of genuine God experiences of which Jesus speaks. What they most seriously misunderstand is that the kind of repentance of which Jesus speaks is not meant to bring us to righteousness, but to the experience of mercy.

We insist upon creating religions based upon righteousness rather than mercy. We want a God who loves righteousness and seeks it rather than mercy within his creation, but this is our conception of God because we want to see ourselves as righteous

---

112. Luke 5:32.

rather than merciful. Jesus' teachings, on the other hand, always point us toward mercy rather than some religious notion of righteousness as defined by right beliefs and behavior. Indeed, mercy clearly seems to be Jesus' notion of righteousness.

Recall the parable of the Good Samaritan with which we began. Jesus was asked by a lawyer, "Who is my neighbor?" Instead of answering that question Jesus gives an example of someone loving his neighbor as himself and therein fulfilling the law. The person he describes is a Samaritan, or someone considered a heretic or religious outsider. He is certainly someone who is not of the same religious tradition as Jesus. But Jesus uses the Samaritan as the example of one who keeps the law by loving his neighbor as himself, and Jesus uses the priest and Levite as examples of those who do not keep the law.[113] As Jesus says, "Go and learn what this means, 'I desire mercy, not sacrifice.' For I have come to call not the righteous but sinners"[114] We want a god who judges us by our standards of righteousness; that is, how well we avoid sin and have the right beliefs and rituals. However, God's judgment is really about how merciful we are. This is why the repentant sinner is in the privileged place of having received much mercy. Jesus always puts the experience of God's mercy above whatever claim to righteousness we might make. He tells us,

> "Two men went up to the temple to pray, one a Pharisee and the other a tax collector. The Pharisee, standing by himself, was praying thus, 'God, I thank you that I am not like other people: thieves, rogues, adulterers, or even like this tax

---

113. Luke 10: 25-37.

114. Matthew 9:13.

> collector. I fast twice a week; I give a tenth of all my income.' But the tax collector, standing far off, would not even look up to heaven, but was beating his breast and saying, 'God, be merciful to me, a sinner!' I tell you, this man went down to his home justified rather than the other; for all who exalt themselves will be humbled, but all who humble themselves will be exalted."[115]

This is why Jesus tells us that "the last will be first and the first last."[116] It is because we, like the older brother in the story of the prodigal, want our righteousness to be valued above the transgressions of our brothers. What we don't understand is the mystery of God's mercy, and how Jesus' teachings are meant to bring us to the experience of that mystery. That, however, is not the Gospel we prefer. We may respond to Jesus' call to repentance, but only if it involves a momentary repentance that leads us back into righteousness. We fail to understand that only perpetual repentance allows us to bask in mercy.

115. Luke 18:10-14.

116. Matthew 19:30; Matthew 20:16; Mark 10:31; Luke 13:30.

CHAPTER NINE

Jesus on Forgiveness and Mercy

WITHOUT A DOUBT, one of the scariest lines in all of scripture is the verse that immediately follows what has come to be known as the Lord's Prayer. When we read it, we should immediately see why it is not included in the Lord's Prayer. Jesus says, "If you forgive others their trespasses, your heavenly Father will also forgive you; but if you do not forgive others, neither will your Father forgive your trespasses."[117] Jesus is telling us in the strongest language possible that our access to the divine is always through forgiveness, and we become more divine only as we grow in forgiveness and mercy. Of course, that is not what we want to hear. We want theologies that tell us how to become divine by becoming righteous and sinless before God. We want theologies that will trump the teachings of Jesus.

There are really only two types of monotheistic religions in the world: those that point us toward righteousness, and those that point us toward forgiveness and mercy. The distinctions between Christians, Jews, Muslims, and Hindus are superficial in comparison to whether the people of those faiths are growing toward becoming more forgiving and merciful or growing toward becoming more righteous. Righteous religions will constantly war with

117. Matthew 6:14-15.

one another over who the truly righteous ones are. Religions based upon righteousness are always tribal religions; the reason for this is because the values that establish what is righteous and what is shameful are always human rather than divine values. The values that Jesus speaks of are so radically divine that two thousand years later we are still not close to hearing his message.

So many people sadly believe that we must gain access to God's presence through the avoidance of sin, having the right theology, or practicing the prescribed rituals, but God's presence is always extended to us through his forgiveness and mercy and in no other way. Likewise, the mystical experience of this forgiveness and mercy is our only real source of security. Of course, without that experience we turn to comprehensive theologies and convince ourselves that our belief systems are our source of security. Our theologies give us something to hold onto, while the experience of God's mercy should bring us to the awareness of someone holding onto *us*. True, our beliefs can provide us with something to grasp onto in order to feel secure, but what we are grasping is a false sense of security.

Consider the story about a man who was caring for his mother when she was in her nineties. In addition to suffering from Alzheimer's, the mother was also blind. Her son would help her down the stairs in the morning to breakfast, and her natural instinct was to want to hold on to him. He would try to explain to her that her holding on to him wasn't going to help if she fell, and she had to trust that he had a solid grip on her. In her demented state, however, she was never able to understand that and always wanted to hold on to him. Similar to a blind person afflicted with Alzheimer's, we also want to hold on to something; in our case, our beliefs, thinking they will save us. But God is always trying to convince us that our only security comes from the experience of *him* holding on to *us*. We need to sense that we are safe and secure and through no effort of our own.

We want it to be about us. We want others to love us because we are good or beautiful, but mercy is the experience of someone loving us because *they* are good and beautiful. We need to be the perpetual recipients of this mercy in order to counteract our illusion that our righteous beliefs or behavior put us in a privileged place. This is the only way to overcome our deepest prejudice that God loves us more than the most despicable of sinners. This is the essential God-experience, and without it, spending eternity in the presence of a merciful God will not be very heavenly. Those who have experienced much mercy will desire to spend eternity with a merciful God, but those who have seen little need for mercy in their life will always resent a God who loves the prodigal as much as the good son. They see a God without limits on his mercy as an unjust God, and it would be tortuous for such *good* people to be forced to spend eternity in the presence of such a God. Thus, even Hell is the result of God's mercy.

The God that Jesus reveals is so foreign and radically divine that we cannot take in his words. It is a God beyond our imagination—a God we cannot comprehend but can only experience, and experience in the midst of our sin. This is why Jesus continually says he came only for sinners and not the righteous. In order to begin to understand Jesus' words, we need to understand the depth of our sin and our enormous need for forgiveness and mercy.

Sadly, most Christian churches have gone in the opposite direction and told us that God wants our holiness to be in terms of righteousness rather than mercy. But Jesus' teachings always privilege mercy over righteousness. Of course, we are called to righteousness as well. Indeed, if we didn't strive for righteousness, there would be no place for repentance and the experience of God's mercy. The call to righteousness, however, is a call to failure. That should be obvious to anyone who really takes seriously Jesus' words. Rightness with God is exemplified in Jesus, and we all fall short of that example and need to repent for the many distractions, attachments, and addictions that keep us from a deeper intimacy and awareness of the Divine presence. That is our great sin: that we do not live as Jesus lived with God in all of our thoughts. If we learn to live in a constant, repentant response to that sin, however, we come to live in the experience of God's mercy. And it is that experience alone that begins to make us into his merciful likeness. We must be forgiven much in order to love as God loves. Jesus says, "The one to whom little is forgiven, loves little."[118]

Most religions focus on making us into righteous objects of love but Jesus' teachings are all about becoming perfect lovers who love the unlovely out of mercy. Jesus consistently stresses the centrality of mercy: "I desire mercy and not sacrifice,"[119] and in Luke's Gospel he says the most beautiful thing.

> "But love your enemies, do good, and lend, expecting nothing in return. Your reward will be great, and you will be children of the Most High; for he is kind to the ungrateful and the wicked. Be merciful, just as your Father is merciful."[120]

118. Luke 7:47.
119. Matthew 9:13; Matthew 12:7.
120. Luke 6:35-36.

"He is kind to the ungrateful and the wicked." We initially hate that about God and want him to respond justly by punishing the wicked and rewarding the righteous; however, none are righteous and all must come to accept God's forgiveness and mercy. We have a lifetime in which to be transformed into people who love forgiveness and mercy. This is what our lives are really all about. God's kingdom is only accessible to those who have become forgiving and merciful. Recall that we began this chapter with one of Jesus' most shocking statements.

> "For if you forgive others their trespasses, your heavenly Father will also forgive you; but if you do not forgive others, neither will your Father forgive your trespasses."[121]

Perhaps the best way to understand this is by imagining that at the end of our lives we meet who we became in our lifetime. That is, that God presents himself to us on our own terms. If throughout our lives we were exacting and demanding people, we meet an exacting and demanding God. If we were forgiving and merciful, we meet a forgiving and merciful God. Indeed, Jesus says, "For with the judgment you make you will be judged, and the measure you give will be the measure you get."[122] Our eternal destiny is based upon who we become and not the dogmas we profess. Jesus never tells us what to believe. As we have said, our doctrines come from his followers and not from Jesus. What Jesus gives us are not doctrines to believe but virtues to develop in preparation for eternal life. What he tells us is that the virtues of his Kingdom are drastically different from the virtues of this

121. Matthew 6:14-15; also see Mark 11:26.
122. Matthew 7:2.

world. We have a lifetime in which to choose the god we love and wish to spend eternity with, but the God that Jesus reveals is so radically different from the tribal gods we imagine that few find the "narrow gate" of which Jesus speaks.

> "Enter through the narrow gate; for the gate is wide and the road is easy that leads to destruction, and there are many who take it. For the gate is narrow and the road is hard that leads to life, and there are few that find it."[123]

Certainly, the road of forgiveness and mercy is hard, but it is the only way to that fullness of life of which Jesus speaks. This is "the way and the truth and the life,"[124] and no one comes to the Father except through the kind of forgiveness and mercy of which Jesus speaks. Sadly, we have interpreted Jesus saying that no one comes to the Father except through him as a matter of having a right theology or believing the right doctrines, instead of seeing the narrow gate as the divine mercy Jesus reveals from the cross. We all want to come to God because of something good within our behavior or our thinking. We hate the idea that God loves all of his creation, and all of that creation is in need of mercy. This is the message of the Gospel that is almost impossible for the righteous to hear. It is easy to think of ourselves as righteous, but difficult for us to imagine that we are perpetually in need of God's mercy.

God has chosen to work through a flaw deep within us to make us into his merciful likeness. As Leonard Cohen's "Anthem" declares, "There is a crack, a crack in everything. That's how the

123. Matthew 7:13-14.

124. John 14:6.

light gets in." Sadly, much of religion is about trying to cover up the crack so we might make a pretense to righteousness. But the truth is that we all come to God through the crack where he meets us with his mercy.

Mercy is more radical than love. Love is affection because of either something good or beautiful in the object of our affection, or something good or beautiful in the one who loves. Mercy, however, is affection toward the very flaws we find within others. God has built a flaw deep within us. He has made us with hearts that are prone to wander, but he has affection even for that, which is what we will never understand but can only experience in order to be made like him in terms of mercy. Mercy is affection for the one who knows that they can't seem to do it right. It is affection for the crippled and crazy, but it is only experienced by those who accept their limp and see their own insane addiction to sin.

We wish to be forgiven once and for all, and have our sins removed through that forgiveness, but it is our sin or thorn in the flesh that keeps us in the perpetual experience of his mercy in order that in time we may become merciful as he is merciful.[125] As we have said, in order to become forgiving and merciful, we must experience forgiveness and mercy on an almost perpetual basis. That is because no one wants to become merciful on their own, since when we extend mercy we enter into the pain of others. Righteous religions give us a way to avoid entering into the pain of others through mercy. We want to believe that others are in pain because they lack the righteousness we possess. Indeed, we want to imagine that God punishes them for their lack of righteousness.

125. 2 Corinthians 12:8.

That is a constant theme with human beings, and we see it running throughout the Biblical revelation.

When we get to Jesus, however, we see something very different. He tells us we are only right with God through God's divine mercy, and we only become like him by becoming merciful. True righteousness, or being right with God, is rooted in our becoming merciful as he is merciful and not our ability to avoid sinful behavior. This is simply too divine for us, so we ignore his teachings and invent theologies that explain the Cross in a way more compatible with our primitive level of human consciousness; in this manner, we avoid ascending to the divine level of consciousness to which Jesus calls us. The Gospel is simply too contrary to who we are as human beings. To embrace it, we need to move to Jesus' level of consciousness, but that level of consciousness requires the destruction of too many of our sacred prejudices. We want a god who allows us to retain those prejudices, which are our true objects of worship. We want to imagine that God has given and sanctioned our religious beliefs, our sense of justice, our wealth, and our love of family. We want a god who looks like us rather than one who shows us how radically different God is from anything human and calls us to take on the mind of Christ and become merciful as he is merciful.

Jesus says, "Go and learn what this means, 'I desire mercy and not sacrifice.' For I have come to call not the righteous but sinners."[126] This seems to be the scripture that unlocks something of the mystery of the Gospel. If Jesus desires mercy and not sacrifice, where will he find it? If mercy is to exist among human beings, it

126. Matthew 9:13.

will be found in those who have received much mercy.

The way we receive much mercy is not by increasing our sinning, but simply by seeing how deep our sin goes and how great our need for mercy is. What others tell us are our virtues, Jesus tells us are our sins. The thing that Jesus preaches most against—even more than religion, justice, wealth, and family—is our hypocrisy or pretense to righteousness.

CHAPTER TEN

Mercy and the Problem of Evil

JESUS' COPERNICAN REVOLUTION of mercy is certainly turning the world upside down. He is presenting us with a concept of God that we are still not ready to fathom. To see just how radical his picture of God is, consider what philosophers and theologians have termed "the problem of evil." It is a logical problem that results from the fact that if God is all-good, all-knowing, all-powerful, and the sole creator of the universe, how do we explain the existence of evil? This creates what logicians call an *inconsistency.* We can resolve the inconsistency by removing any one of the above-mentioned attributes of God. If God were not all-good, there obviously would be evil in the world because of the evil in the creator. Likewise, if God were not all-knowing he could have created a world which he thought would be free of evil without knowing that evil would result from his creation. Or, we could understand God to be less than all-powerful. In Plato's *Timaeus*, the character Timaeus claims that the Demiurge who created the world tried to eliminate all of the preexisting evil but was not powerful enough to do so. Another alternative is to imagine that God was not the sole creator of the universe. According to the ancient Persian religion of Zoroastrianism, there were two creators: one evil and one good, and hence the existence of evil.

Christian orthodoxy has always dealt with this problem by trying to explain evil and suffering in a way that resolves the inconsistency without eliminating any of the divine attributes. Some have argued that evil is only apparent and not ultimately real. Things may appear evil to us but that is to perceive things from our limited perspective: it is to view things in light of what we like or do not like. If we could see things from God's eternal perspective, we would see them very differently. Unfortunately, the result of such a position is that it tends to make us less than compassionate. When people are suffering, if we believe that the evil they suffer is only apparent and not ultimately real, we will tend to lack the essential virtue of compassion. Jesus extended true compassion to people suffering the evil of this world, and he calls us to do the same. A diminished capacity for compassion is a high price to pay for exonerating God as the cause of evil.

Over the centuries, philosophers and theologians have proposed a host of other possible ways to explain or justify the existence of evil, but the one that many find most compelling is the idea of evil as instrumental. The philosopher, John Hick, has written extensively on the idea of evil as a necessary ingredient in God's purpose of making us into his likeness.[127] Hick begins with the Scripture that tells us we are made in the image and likeness of God,[128] but he argues that although we bear the image of God from birth, the likeness of God takes a lifetime to develop. In that process, God uses what we call *evil* as an instrument to that purpose. Thus, just as a medical operation might be painful and undesirable

127. Hick, John. *Evil and the God of Love* (revised edition). New York: Harper & Row, Publishers, Inc. 1977.

128. Genesis 1:26.

in itself, it can have the consequence of restoring us to health, so in like manner God uses evil to make us into his likeness.

Hick, like most people, thinks that God's perfecting of us and making us into his likeness is largely a matter of perfecting our virtues and moral behavior. A different viewpoint is that the perfection that Jesus calls us to is not about becoming what we consider virtuous and moral, but about being made into his forgiving and merciful likeness. Interestingly, if we see our perfection in terms of becoming merciful rather than morally sinless, the existence of evil is very consistent with an all-good, all-knowing, and all-powerful sole creator. If what it means to follow Jesus is a matter of becoming like him in terms of forgiveness and mercy, it makes sense for God to create a world with enormous opportunity to develop those divine virtues. If we are to extend love to sinners and even our enemies[129] through forgiveness and mercy, it follows that God would create a world full of sinners and enemies in order to give us the greatest possible opportunity to develop into his merciful likeness.

Of course, we do not want a God whose purpose for our lives is to transform us into people who can love sinners and enemies. We want God to be the enforcer of divine justice which we imagine is a matter of rewarding good behavior and punishing bad behavior. We want God to be the enforcer of the kind of order we would want if we were God. If we were God, we would base our sovereignty upon power and reward those who obey us and punish those who dare to disobey. The God that Jesus reveals, however, bases his sovereignty upon forgiveness and mercy. The

---

129. Jesus washes the feet of Judas (John 13:2-5), and prays from the Cross that his torturers would be forgiven (Luke 23:34).

Jesus revelation is that of a loving God who desires to instill mercy within his creation. His great purpose behind creation is to create people who, like himself, are able to change others, not through the threat of force, but through forgiveness and love. In order to accomplish that purpose, we must become ever more aware of the mercy he constantly extends to us.

Recall again Jesus saying, "The one to whom little is forgiven, loves little."[130] Conversely, to love much, we must experience much forgiveness. We usually understand this to mean that the one with the greater sin and therefore greater forgiveness will love more, but that is a wrong way to understand the idea of receiving much forgiveness. We are forgetful creatures and no matter how great our offense might be, in no time, we forget its gravity and the grandness of the forgiveness we received. In fact, Jesus relates a story to illustrate this fact. He tells us of an unforgiving servant who, after his master has forgiven him a great deal, did not forgive another who owed him a very small amount.[131] So when Jesus tells us that we must be forgiven much in order to love much, he is not referring to the size of the offense, but rather the frequency of our experience of forgiveness. It is only with the repeated experience of God's mercy that we in time become merciful. As we have said, however, that should not be taken to mean that we are to deliberately sin in order to receive much forgiveness. That is not necessary since Jesus tells us that our sin is much deeper than we imagine and what grieves the heart of God is not our behavior, but the fact that our hearts are prone to wander from an awareness of His presence and the fullness of life that comes with that awareness.

130. Luke 7:47.

131. Matthew 18:23-35.

An awareness of His presence is the essence of prayer, and Jesus' entire life was a prayer. We, however, are constantly diverted from that awareness by the distractions of this world that promise so much yet deliver so little. This is our sin, but the prescription Jesus offers is not what most religious people suppose. It is not that we somehow overcome these distractions and live as Jesus lived in a constant awareness of the Divine presence but that we learn to live in a constant state of repentance. It is only through ongoing repentance and the continual experience of God's mercy that we in time begin to become merciful ourselves.

Thus, theologies that claim that Jesus suffered the offense of our sin, once and for all, and we have no perpetual need of repentance and the ongoing experience of God's mercy, gives us a sense of righteousness but it keeps us from becoming merciful. Repentance and the ongoing experience of mercy is the only path to becoming merciful. God is a suffering God who continues to suffer our rejection of him. Likewise, we continually need to repent and experience his forgiveness for our failure to love God the way Jesus calls us to love with our whole heart, soul, mind, and strength.

Jesus is constantly pointing out that the standard to which God is calling us is much greater than we would like to imagine, and there is a judgment. The judgment is that we have all failed to live the fullness of life that God intends for us. The intention of the judgment, however, is to bring us to repentance in order that we might experience God's mercy. A large part of God's purpose behind creation was to create a species of beings capable of experiencing mercy and therein becoming merciful. Once we understand that, we get a better perspective on the nature of this world and the nature of evil. The greatest opportunity to both experience and extend mercy is in a world ripe with distractions, addictions, and evil. We may find it strange that God would create such a world, but that is because we neither understand God nor his purposes. We would punish the prodigal son and reward the good son.[132] We would punish evil and eliminate those people who were unlike us in their morality or theology. God, however, loves his creation and he even loves what we call evil *so much* that he is able to transform it into mercy. Of course, that doesn't always work and there are times when evil must be destroyed, but God's ultimate desire is always to transform evil into mercy through forgiveness. Henri Nouwen explains it beautifully.

> If evil is seen only as an irreversible, clearly visible, and sharply outlined tumor, then there is only one possibility: cut it out. And then violence is necessary. But when evil is reversible and can be turned into good through forgiveness, then nonviolence becomes possible.[133]

When evil cannot be redeemed, and therefore must be destroyed, it is still an occasion for repentance rather than rejoicing. Even that part of God's creation that cannot be redeemed is still part of his creation, and our destruction of it should be a further opportunity for repentance. Unfortunately, what we most often hear is that God hates evil and the suffering it causes, and obedient followers of God should do everything in their power to oppose and destroy it. What is behind such thinking is that there are bad

132. Luke 15:11-32.

133. Nouwen, Henri. *Encounters with Merton*. New York: Crossroad Publishing, 1981, p. 102.

people (sinners) and good people (who avoid sin), but Jesus lets us know that we are all sinners and should not desire to cast stones. Jesus' notion of holiness is obviously not a matter of sinlessness, given Jesus' concept of sin. Jesus makes it clear that our sin and the evil it breeds are much deeper than we imagine, and no one escapes it. We are all in need of mercy. So holiness is not a matter of avoiding sin, but recognizing our sin and allowing it to bring us to the experience of God's mercy. As we have said, however, in order to increase our experience of mercy we do not have to increase the sin in our lives but only our awareness of the depth of our sin.

All this should not be taken to mean that we are not to oppose evil. Evil is to be opposed, but our opposition to evil should always be with the kind of compassion that mercy entails. The hope and purpose of confronting evil should always be intent upon bringing about the experience of God's mercy both within ourselves and others. In order to do that, we must oppose evil and the suffering it produces in a very different way than that to which human beings have become accustomed. Jesus does not come into the world to destroy evil and suffering, but to show us how to deal with evil in a way that it transforms us into his divine likeness.

God suffers evil and is "kind to the ungrateful and the wicked,"[134] not simply because they are his creation—his beloved sons and daughters—but because God knows that the ungrateful and the wicked might be the very ones with the greatest potential to realize God's ultimate purpose. The greatest sinners make the greatest saints because we really only come to know God, not by doing it right, but by doing it wrong. If the Gospel were about

134. Luke 6:35.

doing it right, there wouldn't be more rejoicing over the one sinner rather than the ninety-nine righteous persons who have no need of repentance.[135]

Our meditations should always focus on the question of whether his mercies are new every morning,[136] and are we living out of that experience, or are we trusting our own understanding to make us righteous and therein oblivious of our constant need of his mercy?

Religions and theologies that focus on righteousness and justice are the great threat to the world, and theologies that make us merciful and forgiving are our only hope. Only a merciful spirituality will save the world. Righteous religion in whatever form continues to destroy it. The religious zealots who believe they have been made righteous through their own theological understanding are further from God than the non-believer who sees the folly in a faith that is based upon our own understanding.

At this point moralists might interject, "So God is OK with mass murderers and those who initiate unjust wars and the suffering that such evil creates?" Of course not, but the Divine reaction to such things is not what we would imagine. God not only created a world that abounds in evil and suffering, but he entered into that evil and suffering in the most dramatic way in order to show us how to become like him in terms of forgiveness and mercy. This is the great mystery of incarnation. As we saw, some atonement theories have tried to end that mystery and explain that the purpose of incarnation was in order for God to punish Jesus for our sins, but the revelation of the Cross is the revelation

135. Luke 15:7.

136. Lamentations 3:2.

of God transforming evil by suffering it and releasing it through forgiveness. This is the revelation of the Cross; those who have taken it seriously and have followed Jesus to their own crosses by suffering evil and releasing it through forgiveness have tasted the divine. For most, however, a God who loves evil so much that he can transform it into love, forgiveness, and mercy is simply beyond their comprehension. It is certainly contrary to the god we create out of our prejudices. What we desire is a god that has our values and our conceptual understanding. This is the god we love and worship: a god that reinforces our sacred prejudices and loves us because we are righteous, industrious, just, and lovers of our families. We want a god with our concept of holiness: holiness founded upon our righteousness rather than mercy.

Rare as it may be, a merciful holiness can still be seen in those individuals who are conscious of the depth of their sin, and consequently live in an almost-constant state of repentance and the experience of God's mercy. These are God's agents of the mercy by which the world continues to be transformed.

CHAPTER ELEVEN

A Second Innocence

THE BIBLE IS God's depiction of God's relationship with human beings. God is the same yesterday, today, and forever, but our relationship with the Divine is greatly dependent upon our level of consciousness, and the conceptual prejudices that make up that level of consciousness; it is through this understanding that we interpret everything. God is willing to meet us where we are in terms of our understanding, but desires that we rise to higher and higher levels of consciousness in order to better understand both the Divine and ourselves. Unfortunately, so many people insist that there is only one level of consciousness: their own. They take their interpretation to be an objective revelation of who God is, in spite of the fact that numerous other interpretations surround them. Their faith is in the conceptual prejudices that make up their level of consciousness. Jesus, however, is introducing us to a level of consciousness that is simply too divine for us. So we either interpret his words through the prejudices of our own understanding, or we ignore his words completely and simply worship him as God.

In order to see the level of consciousness that Jesus is revealing, we must return to a second innocence. In the innocence of our childhood, we received the world as it was presented to us.

That innocence allowed our cultural and linguistic communities to make us into their likeness. We were defenseless against the mind they imposed upon us, and we accepted the way they taught us to conceptualize God, the world, and ourselves. We were wide open to those surrounding influences, and we accepted all the conceptual filters they provided. We were lone children in a world of adults, and they instilled in us their ideas of righteousness—what was right and what was wrong, what we should love and what we should hate. It was unavoidable that we learned their language and their way of being in the world. Their concepts and prejudices became the filters through which we perceived everything. Furthermore, we naively imagined that what we were being taught were things about the world itself rather than merely the way the adults of our social world had been taught to perceive the world. Jesus, however, is calling us to a second innocence.

> "Truly I tell you, unless you change and become like children, you will never enter the kingdom of heaven."[137]

Jesus is telling us that the world from his perspective is very different from the world that we have been taught to see, and if we would like to see the world to which he refers as the *kingdom of heaven*, we need to learn from him, and come to see the world as he sees it. This is what it means to take on the mind of Christ: to have his conceptual understanding, and to interpret the circumstances of our lives as he interpreted the circumstances of his life. This is very different from believing in a doctrine or creed that we have subscribed to as an objective truth. We cannot perceive

---

137. Matthew 18:3.

the Divine objectively, but we can get a better perspective of the Divine if we take on Jesus' concepts of things like sin, repentance, faith, forgiveness, and mercy.

Jesus is telling us that there is another way to perceive the world: a way very different from the one instilled in us in our first innocence. He is calling us to perceive the world as he perceives it. In order to do that, however, we must enter into a second innocence, that is, a place where we allow the concepts which make up his perspective to replace those we acquired from our culture and language community in our first innocence. Jesus is offering us a radically divine perspective, vastly different from the human perspective we initially received. We cannot see this Kingdom of Heaven of which he speaks with our inherited minds. As long as we are confident in our own understanding, we will always mold his teachings to fit that understanding. But it is only by taking on the mind of Christ that we can see and interpret the world as he sees and interprets it.

In our infancy we knew nothing of this world, and thus were fully open to being instructed in the ways of our culture and language community. Jesus, on the other hand, is telling us of a divine world of which we know almost nothing. Only the mind of Christ is capable of seeing that world, but we are kept from that perspective by thinking that we already have the mind of Christ since we were raised in a Christian culture. This notion should be dispelled easily enough by considering, as we have, the things that Jesus has to say about religious righteousness, sin, wealth, justice, family, faith, and mercy.

Jesus is turning the world upside down, and presenting us with a Copernican revolution the likes of which the world has never seen. Unfortunately, what we generally hold as sacred truths are those things we learned in our first innocence. Instead of taking on the mind of Christ, we create theologies that emerge from the mind we inherited.

What Jesus reveals is not a belief system that we profess, but rather a perspective through which to interpret the circumstances of our lives. Since this is a personal perspective rather than a set of doctrines, and we are all in different places in terms of taking on this mind of Christ, we all begin by allowing Jesus' words to do violence to our inherited understanding. It is only then that we can enter into a second innocence and begin the journey to become more like him.